Niwaki

Niwaki

Pruning, Training and Shaping Trees the Japanese Way

Jake Hobson

Timber Press
Portland • London

To Keiko

All illustrations and photographs © Jake Hobson unless otherwise noted. Grateful acknowledgement is made for permission to reprint three lines from *On Love and Barley: The Haiku of Basho*, translated with an introduction by Lucien Stryk (Penguin Classics, 1985). Copyright © Lucien Stryk, 1985.

Mention of trademark, proprietary product or vendor does not constitute a guarantee or warranty of the product by the publisher or author and does not imply its approval to the exclusion of other products or vendors.

Published in 2007 by
Timber Press, Inc.

The Haseltine Building
133 S.W. Second Avenue, Suite 450
Portland, Oregon 97204-3527
timberpress.com

6a Lonsdale Road
London NW6 6RD
timberpress.co.uk

Sixth printing 2014

Designed by Dick Malt
Printed in China

Library of Congress Cataloging-in-Publication Data
Hobson, Jake.
  Niwaki : pruning, training and shaping trees the Japanese way / Jake
Hobson.
    p. cm.
  Includes bibliographical references and index.
  ISBN-13: 978-0-88192-835-8
  1. Ornamental trees–Japan. 2. Ornamental trees–Training–Japan.
  3. Ornamental trees–Pruning–Japan. 4. Gardens, Japanese. I. Title.
  SB435.6.J3H63 2007
  635.9'77–dc22
                        2006033320

A catalog record for this book is also available from the British Library.

Contents

Preface

I first went to Japan with the support of a travel award. I had just graduated from the Slade School of Art in London, where I had been studying sculpture. It was 1996, and I spent one month travelling around the country, ostensibly to study the cultural phenomenon of *hanami*, the cherry blossom season, and the effects it had on people. What I found there, while exploring the temples and parks in search of cherry blossom, was the gardens. At that point in my life I had no interest in gardens or gardening, and I was completely unaware of what Japanese gardens looked like, but I found them fascinating and I vowed to learn more.

The following year I was back, this time with a job teaching English. For a year I spent all my free time exploring, visiting as many gardens as I could, all over the country. During this time I pieced together what it was that so attracted me to these places: it was the trees.

I had grown up in the countryside, and over five years at art school in London I had directed my energy into studying the relationship we have with nature and our environment. The gardens I saw in Japan, and the trees in them, touched me profoundly, and I sought to learn more. I was fortunate enough to meet the Furukawa nursery workers in Osaka, who kindly took me on as a trainee and introduced me to the world of *niwaki*. Once back in England, I started translating what I had learned into practical terms. I found people interested in what I had to say, and soon realized that although Japanese gardens were well documented, there was very little literature on the trees themselves. Writing this book is my attempt to rectify the situation, and to share some of my experiences.

Most of what I have learned has been passed to me by a handful of people in Japan. I owe enormous thanks to Motokazu Furukawa, the entire Furukawa family and everyone I met while working at Furukawa Teijuen. Special thanks also to Futoshi Yoshioka, of the Asuka Noen nursery, for taking so much time and sharing so much with me, and to my brother-in-law, Haruyasu Tanaka (a gardener in Osaka) who has been especially helpful in clearing up some of the mysteries I have encountered along the way. Back in England, the support of Angus White at Architectural Plants, where I worked for six years, has been fantastic, and the shared knowledge and enthusiasm of my friend Jari Eikenaar has been invaluable.

Most of all, for her patience, I want to thank my wife, Keiko. What started off as pleasant garden visits soon turned into fanatical tree-spotting sessions (as they do), with Keiko as my translator, quizzing unsuspecting monks, gardeners and passers-by. Back in England, she might have thought her role was over, but the writing of this book has rekindled her responsibilities. For someone with no more than a passing interest in gardens, she has been patient, helpful and understanding, far beyond the call of duty.

Many thanks are due to Allan Mandell, Jari Eikenaar, and Edzard Teubert, for kindly providing photographs. All the remaining photographic illustrations in the book are my own, many taken long before the idea for a book had been born. I use an old Nikon FE2, normally with a 35 mm lens. I never use a tripod or flash, and always regret not taking better pictures. I have tried, wherever possible, to avoid using well-known gardens as examples, as they appear in many beautifully illustrated books already, and there are so many lesser-known ones still to discover.

Photographing trees is difficult. Catching blossom and autumn colour of course depends a good deal on luck, but the feeling you get from a tree is virtually impossible to capture completely, isolated from its physical setting and reduced to two dimensions. Technical skill, knowledge and appreciation of light all help, but ultimately some shots turn out better than others.

The hand-drawn illustrations are also my own. Despite my art school training, they are not perfect, but they serve their purpose well enough. There is no attempt to achieve realistic botanical impressions, nor should the scale ever be taken too seriously, and the sketches of trees before and after pruning do not always match up. Above all, readers who use these drawings (as I hope many will) should understand that every tree is different, and the drawings are simply a guide from which to work.

Regarding the use of Japanese: I have used the Hepburn system of transliteration, without the macrons over long vowels. In my mind this makes for a more pleasant read, but to those readers proficient in Japanese, I apologize for this simplification. I list people's names in the Western, rather than Japanese way, with given name followed by family name, and all Japanese plant names are taken from a Japanese book called *Nihon no Jyumoku*, or *Woody Plants of Japan* (Yama-kei Publishers 1985).

Finally: I arrived at gardens and *niwaki* by an unusual route (as so many do). I have never studied horticulture, and know nothing much about Western gardening techniques. I have nothing to say about herbaceous borders, roses or lawn mowing. All that I have needed to know, I have picked up along the way; crucially, I have been able to decide for myself what is important (and true), and what is not. This has left me open to influences that some people find difficult to accept as gardening in the conventional sense, but without which there would be no book.

What Are *Niwaki*?

Get a sheet of paper, pick up a pencil, and draw a tree. That is a *niwaki*. It is not living, of course; it's not a real tree. Instead, it is your interpretation—however hastily drawn, however unplanned—of what a tree looks like. It is stylized, a caricature, a stripped-down version of the real thing.

Then take this a step further, and build a tree. It might look like a toy tree flanking a miniature railroad, or like part of a stage set. It probably looks a bit silly, with its features exaggerated—but it is a genuine representation of a tree, however you look at it.

Now take it further still, and actually *grow* a tree. Here you run into trouble; the tree appears to have a mind of its own. It does not look anything like the sketch you drew, or the model you built. Oh, well—it's a living and breathing tree. This is where gardeners in the West tend to stop. "It's a tree; let it get on with it."

Left to grow on its own, it may be as long as half a century before the tree resembles your drawing—half a century, that is, before it bears any resemblance to what you envision a tree to be.

For the Japanese, however, the process of growing a garden tree is not wholly unlike sketching or building one. Observations, memories, emotions and thousands of years of cultural and practical tradition inform Japanese gardeners and nursery workers as they cultivate their garden trees, coaxing out those features believed to signify 'the essence of tree': gnarled trunks, outstretched branches, rounded canopies. The process of cultivating the garden tree can be thought of as a continuation of the model and of the drawing—one more step towards expressing what it is that defines the tree. Translated literally: *niwaki* are, quite simply, garden trees.

'The essence of tree': gnarled trunks, outstretched branches and rounded canopies. Zenko-ji, Nagano. (Photo by Jari Eikenaar)

Regions and prefectures of Japan

Tohoku Region
Akita
Aomori
Fukushima
Iwate
Miyagi
Yamagata

Kanto Region
Chiba
Gumma
Ibaraki
Kanagawa
Saitama
Tochigi
Tokyo

Chubu Region
Aichi
Fukui
Gifu
Ishikawa
Nagano
Niigata
Shizuoka
Toyama
Yamanashi

Kinki
Hyogo
Kyoto
Mie
Nara
Osaka
Shiga
Wakayama

Chugoku Region
Hiroshima
Okayama
Shimane
Tottori
Yamaguchi

Shikoku Island
Ehime
Kagawa
Kochi
Tokushima

Kyushu Island
Fukuoka
Kagoshima
Kumamoro
Miyazaki
Nagasaki
Oita
Saga

Adapted from Ran Levy-Yamamori and Gerard Taaffe,
Garden Plants of Japan (Timber Press, 2004).

Topography of Japan

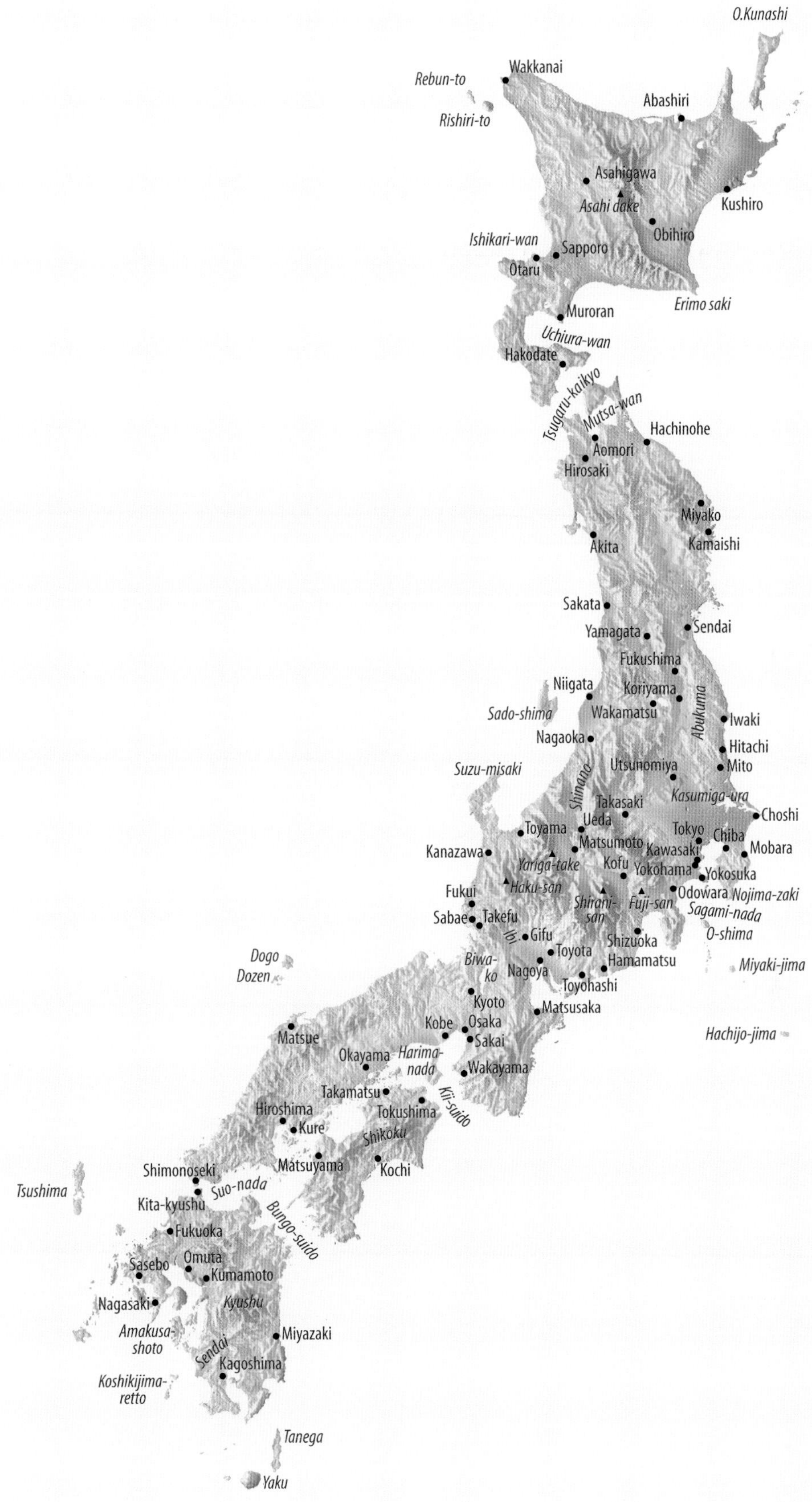

Elements of the garden.
Reiun-in, Kyoto.

1
Garden Elements

Japanese gardens evoke landscapes, in more ways than one. Inspired by the mountains, riverbeds, streams and waterfalls that pervade the country, they refer to physical landscapes. Yet they can also be thought of as abstract landscapes—landscapes of the subconscious, influenced by Buddhism and Shinto spirituality and shaped by ancient mores.

Various elements combine to create the garden as a whole. Visually, the strongest and most familiar of these elements are the rocks, water and ornaments such as lanterns and pagodas. Loaded with symbolism, cultural meaning and tradition in their home country, they are generally seen by Western gardeners as the key features of Japanese gardens. They appear exotic and attractive, their strong images enduring in the memory. Used with subtlety and understanding, they can be vital components of the garden; when, for instance, a pagoda emerges from among plants like a hilltop temple, or a bridge suggests a crossing point in a mountain stream, these elements augment the garden's landscape, giving it a human dimension.

There is a danger, however, that when Japanese-style gardens are created outside of Japan, these defining features may become, at best, mere pastiche, confused and misinterpreted. At worst, they can look downright tacky; they are surprisingly difficult to master, and when used carelessly they risk slipping into the realm of the garden gnome. A true Japanese garden is rooted in its surroundings, both physically and culturally, and the elements it includes are very much the product of those surroundings. Removed from the physical and cultural background to which they belong, such ornaments lose their significance and become nothing more than decoration. For a more authentic approach to Japanese-style gardening, Westerners would do well to look beyond this decoration, seeking out elements that are intrinsically linked not just to the garden, but to the landscape itself.

The most elusive, indefinable and thus most often overlooked element in the Japanese garden is its trees: the *niwaki*. Trees are the sole features of the Japanese garden that—regardless of the cultural values attached to them—are truly universal, in that they are living, breathing things. (Water, rocks and gravel, despite existing all over the world, carry the significant baggage of Buddhist and Shinto symbolic value.)

A visit to any temple garden in Japan, a walk through the suburban back streets of any town, or the view from any train windows will attest to the significance of the country's trees. They are everywhere. Even the most minimalistic temple gardens, such as Ryoan-ji in Kyoto, rely on trees; there, although none are present within the courtyard walls, the backdrop to the sea of raked gravel and rocks beyond the walls is heavily planted with cedar and flowering cherry, serving as a foil to the scene below. The reliance on trees and plants is no different from most other gardening cultures in the world, climate permitting. What *is* different, however, is how the trees look. Trees in Japanese gardens, the *niwaki*, are trained, shaped, clipped and pruned to fit into the landscape of the garden in a way that is peculiar to Japan.

The source and inspiration for Japanese gardens can be traced to three fundamental factors: the country itself (its landscapes, geography and climate), the religious beliefs (Shinto and Buddhism), and the cultural aesthetics of Japan. These sources are inextricably linked, and have to be thought of together to get a decent overall picture of the gardens.

Cryptomeria-clad mountains make up much of Japan's landscape.

Coastal plains, Shikoku. Every inch of land is used.

Nature

Japan is a long, thin country, extending from Hokkaido in the north down to Okinawa, which reaches almost as far south as Taiwan. The country is actually an archipelago, with the four main islands—Hokkaido, Honshu, Shikoku and Kyushu—extending from north to south. Honshu, home to Tokyo and Kyoto, is where the majority of the gardens mentioned in this book are to be found.

Hills or mountains cover 80 per cent of the country; they range from the soaring alps to the crumpled, interlocking hills that can be seen on any train journey. All but the highest peaks are covered in dense forest, most of which is managed for timber, swathes of *Cryptomeria japonica* and *Chamaecyparis obtusa* planted among broadleaved woodland. Wherever you are in Japan, you are never far from the hills.

Because of the mountainous landscape, inhabitable land is scarce. Most of the population (around 126 million) live on the coastal plains. Cities such as Tokyo, Yokohama and Kawazaki, on the Kanto plain, are individual cities only in name, so dense is the population throughout their shared territory. Even in earlier times, with smaller populations, the coastal plains were crowded. Visitors to Japan confirm many of their preconceptions about crowded cities without ever getting the chance to explore the less populated countryside, although even here land management is intense, with every scrap of land put to use. Rice fields and vegetable patches compete with convenience stores and car parks, resulting in a highly worked patchwork landscape.

Stretching over 20 degrees of latitude, Japan's climate is complex. The influence of continental Asia to the west, and the

Pacific Ocean to the east, results in well-defined weather patterns and distinct seasons. The Japanese psyche is highly attuned to seasonal change, which is celebrated in the media and the arts across the country. Deciduous and flowering trees with strong seasonal interests are loaded with symbolism of life, the passing of time and natural progression.

Spring starts with *haru ichiban*, the first winds of spring, in March. This witnesses the Japanese apricot blossom, followed by the cherry blossom in April and the azalea blossom in May. It is an exciting time in the garden, and traditionally the best time to visit Japan.

Before the transition from spring to summer comes the rainy season in June, when for four weeks or so a warm, grey drizzle blankets the country. The rains signal the preparation and planting of the rice paddies, and are stronger further south. Hokkaido in the north escapes the rains, having a longer winter and later spring. In the gardens, the moss that has dried out over the winter leaps back into life, trees put on their first flush of growth, and everything is a vigorous, luminous green. If you can bear the muggy weather, it is a fantastic time to visit; *Hydrangea macrophylla* and *Rhododendron indicum* are in flower, and the tour buses full of school children have disappeared with the end of spring.

Summer brings a blistering, humid heat, and air conditioning, especially in the cities, is essential. The gardens are alive with the screech of cicadas, the rice fields heave with the nocturnal chorus of frogs, and the constant whine of mosquitoes accompanies the evening cool.

The summer months see a lot of action in the garden, with everything growing furiously. Gardeners with broad-brimmed straw hats, or towels wrapped around their heads, are a

Intensively worked countryside. Shikoku.

By late summer, gardens can be in need of attention. Raikyu-ji, Takahashi.

Spring in Kyoto.

common sight, often resting in the shade during the heat of the day (lunch breaks are longer in the summer). Once, when I was working for Furukawa nursery near Osaka, it was so hot that by eight-thirty in the morning, after just half an hour of simple work, I had worked up such a sweat that my trousers sloshed with every step I took, and needed to be wrung out like laundry.

Some gardens can look rather neglected in the height of summer. Gardeners tend to visit at set times of the year, when they carry out a major overhaul of the garden, rather than making short, regular visits. By the autumn, when most gardens are due to be tidied up, some of the trees are starting to lose their shape and definition, but this somehow feels appropriate in the heat.

The end of summer is announced by a brief, wet, typhoon season, that is more intense further south. The typhoons, which are numbered rather than named, race across the Pacific from the Equator, causing damage from the speeding winds and heavy rains that they bring. Despite bringing a good deal of problems, though, they do seem to blow the summer humidity away.

Autumn is the most comfortable season in Japan. The rains die down, the heat has gone, but the cold winter winds have yet to arrive. Autumn colour, particularly vivid in the maple trees, creates scenes as compelling as spring cherry blossom and just as popular with the crowds. On television there is a daily report on the progress of the *koyo*, the changing leaf colour, just after the weather forecast. Seasonal food appears—chestnuts, pumpkins, certain fish—and the *kaki* (*Diospyros kaki*) ripen on the trees as the leaves drop.

The garden is busy at this time of year. All trees are pruned and tidied up for the winter, sharpening the outlines in the garden as if the view had come into focus through a camera

Autumn in Yamagata Prefecture.

Below: The landscapes of Japan, reproduced in an abstract form. Myoren-ji, Kyoto.

A dusting of snow defines the sculptural qualities of these pines. Zenko-ji, Nagano.
(Photo by Jari Eikenaar)

lens. Clipping and thinning at this time of year also prevents the winter cold from damaging any late summer growth that may not have ripened fully. Pine trees are treated to a rigorous, time-consuming process known as *momiage*, where all the old needles are plucked by hand, leaving only the newest, freshest foliage on the tree. It is a fascinating opportunity for visitors to Japan to observe some of these skills and techniques in action. Visit in October or November and you are bound to come across gardeners at work, either in the temple gardens or high up on ladders, peeking out from behind the walls of private residences.

Winter tends to be cold and dry on the east side of the country, while heavy snow defines the west coast and central mountainous areas, especially further north. It is usually fresh, clear and sunny, and activity in the gardens continues until the New Year, by which time the gardeners hope to have finished their work.

Japan is one of the most seismically active countries in the world. It experiences an average of one thousand earthquakes every year—mostly minor tremors, but some deadly in their strength. Tokyo was virtually destroyed in 1923 by one such earthquake and the fires that followed. More recently, Kobe suffered in 1995. In addition to earthquakes there are forty mountains currently classed as active volcanoes, and the same tectonic faults that cause these volcanoes and earthquakes are also responsible for *tsunami*, the tidal waves caused by earthquakes out at sea.

The constant threat of danger, in particular of earthquakes, has instilled a great sense of acceptance into the Japanese people; the earthquakes bring destruction, then people rebuild and continue much as before. The rewards to be had from the country itself seem to outweigh the disadvantages, and have helped to form a national character highly in tune with its surroundings.

In short, Japan is a mountainous country, surrounded by coastline and covered in trees, rocks, rivers and waterfalls. Its people have traditionally depended on the whims of their climate for survival, accepting the problems of earthquakes and volcanoes as a necessary evil. This is a country that demands a huge amount of respect from its inhabitants, people who even

Sand cone representing Mount Fuji. Ginkaku-ji, Kyoto.

Below: The depth and texture of *Juniperus chinensis* 'Kaizuka' suggest a landscape of hills and valleys, shrouded in cloud.

today remain connected to the land, respectful of it yet thankful for its beauty and abundance.

One needs only a very basic knowledge of the landscapes of Japan to appreciate how directly the gardens are influenced by the country's physical geography. Rocks, streams, riverbeds and waterfalls appear everywhere in the mountains, and are reproduced in gardens all over the country. The mountains themselves provide the fundamental form of many gardens, in the shape of mossy hillocks reduced in scale. The raked gravel of temple gardens could be interpreted at a literal level as stony riverbeds or the ocean, and the use of native trees from surrounding woodland forges a clear link between the wild landscape and the manmade gardens.

Individual features are sometimes directly traceable to their source. The large sand cones seen in several gardens, most famously at Ginkaku-ji, the Silver Pavilion, are clearly based on Mount Fuji, whose presence as a national symbol makes it instantly recognizable. As an iconic image of Japan it is repro-

duced everywhere, especially in the media. It is no coincidence that while the defining British icon is probably the Queen or Big Ben, and in the United States the Statue of Liberty, Japan is represented by Mount Fuji, a natural feature.

The connection between *niwaki* and the wider landscape is palpable, even to those with no real knowledge of Japan. There is a certain feel to nature, present all over the temperate world—a primeval, elemental force that transcends boundaries—and *niwaki* often echo this feeling. Trees in gardens can evoke feelings of cloud-covered mountains and deep forests, isolated cliff-top trees or the majesty and maturity of prime specimens. They can represent just one individual tree, but they can also suggest entire landscapes.

Left: *Shimenawa* detail.

Right: *Shimenawa* around an old specimen of *Cryptomeria japonica*. Kasuga Taisha, Nara.

Faith as Inspiration

In the garden, references to the wider landscape only become truly interesting when considered alongside the culture and spirituality of the Japanese people. These more abstract elements imbue the physical world with a poetic sense of symbolism and meaning, combining to give the gardens and trees deeper resonance and adding layers of significance that nature alone—without human intervention—does not provide.

Shinto

Shinto, 'the way of the gods', is the national religion of Japan. It places great emphasis on life, manifesting itself not only at births and marriages, but also at activities such as the growing of crops, and the construction and opening of new buildings. It is also deeply bound up with gestures of cleansing and purification, evoked by the sweeping of gravel areas at shrines, and, most famously, the complete rebuilding of the main shrine in the country, Ise-jingu, every twenty years. (It was last rebuilt in 1993.)

Shinto arose from the beliefs of the indigenous people, who created myths to help explain the origins of Japan. It involves strong elements of Shamanism, particularly nature worship. Mountains, rivers, rocks and trees—old, exceptionally large or unique in form—are thought to be abodes of the gods (*kami*), and are considered sacred. There is one Shinto myth, first researched by Nobuzane Tsukushi in 1964, that seems particularly relevant to the history of gardens.

As the myth goes, the sun goddess used to make a yearly descent from the heavens in the Ise region of Mie Prefecture, where the people of Ise would bring her down from the mountains in the form of a tree trunk, leaving it on the gravelly riverbank overnight to bring new life for the coming year. The tree was fenced off with rope, marked as a sacred area. In his *Japanese Gardens* (1993), Gunter Nitschke notices the connection between this myth, Shinto shrines, and the development of the garden in Japan, where the use of gravel clearly has symbolic resonance.

The tying of rice straw rope (known as *shimenawa*, literally meaning 'tighten rope') around trees and rocks to mark out sacred boundaries is a common practice at Shinto shrines today, continuing the tradition that arose with the Ise myth. Rocks and old trees, in shrines as well as in the mountains, have this rope tied around them, but the influence does not stop there. In the garden, the art of tying, wrapping and binding lives on in various practical aspects. Form and function are combined; traditional techniques and materials are used with great skill and beauty to protect and secure plants.

Each winter, to protect against the heavy snowfalls that the north of Japan receives, remarkable structures known as *yukit-suri* are built around trees. Large maypole-like contraptions are raised above individual trees, from which hundreds of lengths of rice fibre rope are hung, supporting the weight of branches below. The amazing pine trees at Kenrokuen in

Wigwam *yukitsuri* around *Taxus cuspidata*, awaiting the snow. Niigata.

Below: An old cherry tree, its trunk protected from the elements. Kyoto.

Ishikawa Prefecture are particularly well known for this treatment, but all trees in areas of heavy snowfall receive similar attention, from the most mundane hedges and municipal planting to the most impressive garden trees. Sometimes wigwam structures are built to help shed the snow, remaining in place until all chances of snow have gone. (This winter, as I sit writing in England, I hear from friends that Yamagata city, in the north of the country, has 60 cm [24 in.] of snow, and the surrounding mountains receive up to 3 m [10 ft.] during a typical winter.)

Tender plants such as the sago palm are wrapped up using a technique called *waramaki*, where straw skirts are drawn up around the trunks and foliage, then capped off with a pointed hat. These structures remain in place all winter, and they form remarkable sights, like communities of tall, thin, grass-roofed huts, almost with a life of their own.

These various structures are all exquisitely made, with natural materials such as the rice fibre rope and bamboo poles. Given that they are present in the garden for three months or more, it is understandable that they are well made, but the attention to detail and the resulting sculptural forms go far beyond the call of duty, adding another level of interaction between people and nature to the garden. The results have much in common with the landscape-based projects of the sculptor Christo, who wraps objects, including trees, in materials such as hessian, canvas and plastic, hiding their true exterior and instead revealing new qualities in form and surface. The influence of Shinto, whether recognized or not, is fundamental in this attitude towards material and technique, and should not be underestimated. (Tying and wrapping as a practical art is also seen in the rootballing of trees when they are sold from

Heian-jingu, Kyoto.

the nurseries. Although this handicraft gets buried soon after it is done, only to rot down in the earth, it is fascinating to see the skill and care with which it is carried out.)

Shinto could be said to have given the Japanese people their deep respect for nature, although of course Shinto itself was born of that same respect; one did not necessarily give rise to the other. Certainly from the point of view of the gardens, the influence of Shinto, and the reverence for nature it inspired in people, cannot be underestimated. Recently, in contemporary garden making, there has been strong interest in wilder, more natural styles of garden, using a lot of the plants traditionally associated with Shinto. The native evergreen forests of the southern half of Japan, known as *shoyojurin*, are a renewed source of inspiration to designers, with less commonly used native trees becoming popular.

The most important Shinto shrine in Japan is Ise-jingu (Ise Shrine), in Mie Prefecture. It dates back to the third century, although in keeping with tradition the 200 buildings are completely replaced every twenty years. The most impressive shrine garden is probably Heian-jingu in Kyoto. Famous for its weeping cherries and stone pillar stepping-stones, it was built in 1894, modelled on eighth-century designs.

Ultimately, though, Shinto's real influence is evident not in the gardens themselves, but more in the general respect that the Japanese people have for nature. Meiji-jingu, in Tokyo, built to commemorate the emperor Meiji and his wife, has no garden to speak of, but instead has a large area of woodland park. The planting, completed in 1920, consisted of a range of native trees, including faster-growing *Pinus* species and *Cryptomeria japonica*, as well as slower evergreens such as *Castanopsis* species and *Quercus* species. The plan for the

woodland was that it would originally be closed to visitors (as the most sacred Shinto land often is), and untouched by human hands. Parts of it are now open to the public, but the wardens have a strict hands-off policy, and nothing is allowed to leave the park. The evergreens have now established themselves in a natural order of regeneration, giving the impression of virgin woodland. Considering that the shrine buildings are reproductions (the originals were destroyed during World War II) and this woodland is all that remains of the original shrine, it is all the more inspiring to think that since 1920, naturally regenerating woodland has thrived in the heart of Tokyo.

Buddhism

Buddhism came to Japan from China and Korea in the sixth century. It had an enormous effect on Japan and its people, who demonstrated their remarkable ability to assimilate new ideas into their own culture without losing their original integrity. For most of the time since, Shinto and Buddhism have coexisted successfully, with elements of Shinto present in Buddhist temples, and vice versa.

Buddhism introduced people to a new way of thinking, bringing about new attitudes towards life and death. Temples were built, in which monks made gardens as vehicles for their contemplation. Myths such as the island of the immortals, known as *Horai san* in Japan, provided inspiration, resulting in the landscape of ponds and islands that define many Japanese gardens. In turn, the abstract thought of Zen Buddhism introduced raked gravel and rocks to represent a more introspective view of life, although interestingly the idea of a Zen garden is a Western one, first coined as recently as 1935 by the American writer Loraine Kuck. (This use of gravel

Pinus parviflora, **used to create a sense of infinite space. Daisen-in, Kyoto.**

was inherited from the early Shinto shrines, but used in a more creative, abstract manner in the Zen temples.)

Buddhism's effect on *niwaki* is significant. The new attitudes and awareness towards life and death resulted in a shift in scale of the garden, not physically but symbolically, encompassing the new ideas and beliefs. Trees became a vital tool in this new sense of metaphysical scale; like rocks and gravel, they conveyed the sense of vast landscapes disappearing into infinity. In countless gardens the scale and positioning of trees is cleverly organized to imply this infinite scale of the universe, yet in others a single tree is all that is needed to capture abstract symbolic thought.

Also influential is the Buddhist trilogy of heaven, man and earth, manifested in various ways in the arts of Japan, most famously in the rock formations in the garden, known as *sanzonseki*. Heaven (*ten*) is expressed through a tall, vertical rock, while earth (*chi*) is usually a low, flat one with a strong horizontal emphasis. Man (*jin*), the link between heaven and earth, is the diagonal element firmly rooted to the earth but looking up to the heavens. From this has sprung the Japanese aesthetic of odd numbers and irregular balance that presents such a contrast to the classical aesthetics of Europe. Tree groupings and *ikebana* (flower arranging) are influenced by this trilogy as much as rock placement, the seemingly random arrangements actually underpinned by rigid symbolic guidelines.

The majority of gardens open to the public are in Buddhist temples. (Shinto shrines, royal palaces and parks, and one or two public gardens make up the rest.) Many are gathered in Kyoto, but wherever you are in Japan, you will never be far from a temple, and most of them have some sort of garden, whose attraction often lies in its simplicity and remoteness.

Temples are usually signified by the ending *-ji*, such as Ryoanji, while sub-temples within larger complexes have the ending *-in*. Shinto shrines end with *-jingu*.

Culture as Inspiration

Having looked at the geographical and spiritual inspiration behind the gardens, it is important to consider the social and cultural environment in which they were, and still are, created. The traditional arts of theatre, landscape painting, poetry, pottery, flower arranging and garden design exist as one aesthetic, inseparable from one another. First, though, the early influence of China must be taken into account. Much of Japan's culture was introduced from China, most importantly Buddhism and the Chinese writing system. Of particular importance to the garden, especially in its early stages of development, was *fengshui*.

Fengshui

The influence of *fengshui*, the Chinese philosophy of geomancy, was a strong factor in the development not just of the garden, but also of society in general. The layouts for towns and palaces were based around certain auspicious spatial concepts: the ideal location faced mountains to the north and was flanked by a river to the east, a main highway to the west and a pond or lake to the south. On a large scale, Kyoto, built as the new capital in 794 AD, was laid out along these guidelines, with the Imperial palace also facing north in the centre of the city.

As the Chinese influence was assimilated, the rigid structures of *fengshui* were relaxed, functioning more as guidelines than as strict rules. In garden making in particular, when it

The three rocks at the back of the courtyard represent heaven, man and earth. Ryogen-in, Kyoto.

was not always practical to work within such strict confines, alternatives were found. For instance, trees began to replace certain geographic features in order to achieve the same auspicious effects. There seems to be some flexibility in these alternatives; the two major texts drawn upon by garden historians differ somewhat in their instructions.

Tachibana no Toshitsuna, the eleventh-century courtier and poet, wrote the garden manual *Sakueti-ki*, an important record of aesthetics at the time. In it, he specifies that the highway to the west could be replaced symbolically by seven maples, three cypress trees (probably *Cryptomeria japonica* or *Chamaecyparis obtusa*) could replace the mountains to the north, nine willows could be substituted for the river to the east and nine Judas trees (perhaps *Cercidiphyllum japonicum* rather than *Cercis chinensis*) could serve for the pond to the south. This seems practical advice, with the trees listed in their natural habitats, although the reason behind the specific numbers is never provided. (They are, however, all odd numbers, as is usually the case with Japanese planting, where natural irregularities and asymmetry are favoured over even numbers and regular symmetry.)

Contrastingly, in a manual known as *Illustrations For Designing Mountain, Water and Hillside Field Landscapes*, the fifteenth-century priest Zoen makes no direct reference to the substitution of *fengshui*. However, he recommends, in point 49, that "you should plant willows to the northwest, maples to the northeast, pines to the southeast, and cryptomerias to the southwest".

The ability to glean useful information, to assimilate it into one's own criteria, is obviously important in dealing with strict structures such as *fengshui*, and the Japanese took what they needed, reinterpreting it to fit in with their own sensibilities. Tellingly, point 48 of the *Illustrations* had already explained that "trees from hills and fields are to be planted in the hills and fields of the garden, trees from deep mountains are to be planted on the large mountains, and trees from villages are to be planted in village settings"—a truly apt description of *niwaki* in general, and one that has underpinned the planting of all gardens since.

The Arts

The Japanese arts, such as theatre, landscape painting, ceramics, poetry, the tea ceremony, flower arranging and garden design, all share one common source, one aesthetic. At the core of this aesthetic is a respect for nature, shaped by Shinto and Buddhism, combined with the respect and appreciation for the human touch. Hisamatsu (1971) defines seven characteristics shared by all Japanese arts, inspired specifically by Zen Buddhism: asymmetry, simplicity, austere sublimity, naturalness, subtle profundity, freedom from attachment, and tranquillity. The Japanese terms *wabi* and *sabi* sum up this elusive collaboration: the raw purity of nature (its beauty living side by side with imperfection and harsh reality) is combined with man's creative and spiritual intervention, refining nature down to an essence. Much has been written on *wabi sabi*, and I direct you towards the safe hands of Andrew Juniper's book *Wabi Sabi: The Japanese Art of Impermanence* (2003) for further guidance. Regarding *niwaki*, *wabi sabi* can perhaps be detected in the atmosphere that trees (particularly pines) can create, and the sense of melancholy they can evoke, especially when they are trained to represent old, weather-torn specimens.

Man's touch, the proof of his presence, is a feature of Japanese aesthetics as much as a sense of truth and respect for

Pinus densiflora **evoking the melancholy of** *wabi sabi*. **Kyu-Furukawa teien, Tokyo.**

Below: Splints, supports and guy ropes training a young *Pinus thunbergii*. **Kosho-ji, Uchiko.**

materials. The forge marks on the very best kitchen knives and garden tools serve to remind us of the maker's skills, while in the garden the bamboo poles and scaffolding used to support trees are not hidden, but instead turned into something of great beauty as well as functionality. Likewise the heavy pruning and thinning of trees, seemingly at odds with nature but also inextricably linked, is not disguised, but celebrated.

The landscape ink painting style that came from China, in particular from the Northern Song Dynasty (960–1127 AD) was initially of great importance as inspiration to early garden makers in Japan. It was of particular significance to the Buddhist monks, whose designs reflected their interpretations of the scrolls they received from the continent. These artistic interpretations of mountainous landscapes featured great depth and distorted perspective, and the stylized representation of trees, especially pines, must have served as inspiration for Japanese gardens. However, the matter of how much influence came from the paintings, rather than from the landscape itself, is debatable. Fine examples of Northern Song landscape painting can be seen at the Metropolitan Museum of Art in New York City and the British Museum in London.

Personally, as someone with a fair knowledge of Japanese culture who has travelled over much of the country, I feel that although a broad awareness of the cultural and spiritual influences provides a better understanding with which to appreciate the gardens (as is the case with all intelligent tourism) what is most important of all, from a Western point of view, is an open mind and a willingness to look. I now realize how lucky I was to have discovered Japan and its gardens before I became interested in gardening back home in England. With fresh eyes and an open mind, I was able to see things without judgement or expectations, and to decide for myself what really mattered. Louis Aragon, the surrealist poet and French resistance fighter, noted that "nature is our subconscious". I interpret this to mean that deep down within all of us is an inherent capacity to appreciate nature; rational explanation, in my view, is less important than this most basic sense.

Cycas revoluta, native to the
warmer, southern parts of
Japan.

2
The Roots of *Niwaki*

Remarkably, the range of plants used in Japanese gardens over the last 1500 years has seen very few changes, despite the gardens' evolution over the ages. The tradition of garden making developed in and around Kyoto, the imperial and cultural capital (although not always the political one) from 794 AD. The plants used in these early gardens were all natives, not just to Japan but also to the local hills immediately surrounding Kyoto. Although the term *niwaki* now encompasses all trees used in the gardens, whether native or exotic, it previously referred specifically to the Kyoto natives. Nowadays, gardeners in Japan simply say *achi no ki*, literally meaning 'tree over there', to refer to exotics from abroad.

The hills around Kyoto were covered with a mixture of conifers, evergreens and deciduous trees. Trees from outside this fairly small area were known as *zoki*, and tended to come from either the cooler north (*Taxus cuspidata*) or from the warmer south (*Cycas revoluta*). For many years exotics from abroad were simply not used, and even today they can appear unusual, looking out of place among the locals. *Trachycarpus fortunei* and *Cedrus deodara* are two of the most common imports; they are used in gardens frequently enough not to stand out, but it is rare to see even these species in many traditional temple gardens.

It could be argued that Japan's wealth of botanical riches explains Japanese gardeners' disinclination to look elsewhere. This is true, but it does not give the full story. The *niwaki* and *zoki* sit comfortably in the landscape, and I believe that a deep appreciation for this sense of belonging explains why Japan's gardeners are so devoted to their native specimens. In the Japanese garden it is vital that the overall effect be cohesive, and that it form part of the landscape's natural balance;

Successful immigrants,
Trachycarpus fortunei (right)
and ***Cedrus deodara*** (below).

Left: *Podocarpus macrophyllus*, "after pruning into proper tree form". Kyoto.

Desirable characteristics of the mountains (right) reproduced in the garden (below).

accordingly, gardens have always reflected the surrounding landscapes, conjuring up views and atmospheres to reflect and complement them. The dense tree-covered mountains, streams and waterfalls, cliffs and coastlines were re-created in Japan's gardens, and the corresponding trees from those landscapes were employed. What use would a fancy exotic be, if it failed to ignite any sentiment in the viewer? Translating *The Tsurezuregusa of Kenko*, a fourteenth-century work of medieval Japanese literature, scholar Donald Keene gets straight to the point (1967): "As a rule, oddities and rarities are enjoyed by persons of no breeding. It is best to be without them."

So although an early definition of *niwaki* was of plants that grew in the Kyoto area, the term has now broadened, and refers to all trees (and woody shrubs) grown in gardens. What really defines *niwaki*, though, is *how* they are grown. Kitamura and Ishizu (1963) repeatedly describe trees being used in the garden "after pruning into a proper tree form". This is a very telling comment, and one that effectively sums up *niwaki* in one line, marking out the distinction between a naturally occurring tree in the wild, and a garden tree transformed by human hands into a 'proper' shape.

Little is known about Japanese gardens in general before around 522 AD, when Buddhism arrived from China. Even less is known of the trees that might have been used in those gardens. The history of the *niwaki* really begins with the introduction of Buddhism, which runs parallel to the introduction of the garden (in the modern sense of the word).

Heavily influenced by their Chinese counterparts, the makers of these early Japanese gardens sent workers out into the mountains to find suitable trees. They would be looking for specimens which were small enough to move, but which had

enough character to add a sense of maturity to the garden. These trees were then tidied up in the garden, and from then on pruned and shaped by the new gardeners. They sought out features that would give the trees character: gnarled trunks that were bent and buckled by the wind, widespread branches, and interesting outlines. Trees growing on cliffs and exposed mountain sides, or those growing deep in the shade of forests, or in the open in sheltered areas, would all have their own desirable characteristics.

Right from the start Japanese gardens were conceived of as microcosms of the wider landscape, and the transplanted trees were chosen for their small stature. To keep them at that miniaturized scale, certain pruning techniques were developed, many of which essentially mimicked the natural elements that had created the trees in the first place. This very practical objective of keeping a tree at a certain size is fundamental to *niwaki*; early gardeners looked to nature for guidance as they developed pruning techniques to contain trees within the garden. Although it is unclear when the first nurseries (as we know them now) were started, it would be fair to assume that

as the demand for domestic trees grew, so too did the art of growing *niwaki* in the nursery (rather than adopting them from the wild).

Terminology

In the West, the terminology that has evolved to talk about *niwaki* is muddled and confusing. Whereas the term *bonsai* has been accepted, and is largely understood by most gardeners, most people's grasp of any Japanese garden feature beyond flowering cherries and Japanese maples is slim. Attempts have been made to expand awareness, with expressions like 'big *bonsai*' offering a passable description of some *niwaki*. Yet when used in this sense, the term 'big *bonsai*' overlooks the fundamental definition of *bonsai* (literally, 'potted tree'): that it is grown in a pot. *Niwaki*, as their name suggests, are grown in the ground, and this is the vital difference between the two. Interestingly, though, both *bonsai* and *niwaki* are grown to achieve the same objective: to capture and represent the essence of what being a tree is all about. On the smaller trees, the styles and terminology are more varied, and the gardener often works with more care and attention to detail; however, at heart the two forms set out to do the same thing, and so are vitally similar.

Recently the term 'cloud pruning' has been used to describe various Japanese and non-Japanese effects, albeit in a very vague way. There is no style or term in Japanese that directly translates as 'cloud pruning', although *edabukishitate* uses the verb *fuku*, to blow or puff (*eda* means 'branch', and *fuku* turns to *buki*) but even this is by no means the definitive style,

and to the Western eye no more resembles clouds than many other styles. In England, the term is often used to describe the great billowing, organic hedges of *Taxus baccata* or *Buxus sempervirens* that are to be found in old country houses, and in the modern topiary of designers like Jacques Wirtz. This would appear to be an accurate description, but bears little resemblance to the Japanese *edabukishitate* style, having much more in common with the clipped azalea *karikomi*.

The term 'Japanese topiary' sounds suitable, although many in the West associate topiary with a formal style, and might be unable to grasp the connection between topiary and the natural landscape. The term 'pom-pom' is also used, but conjures up images of poodles and lollipops, in a very decorative manner. The only term that does justice to the range of styles and techniques seen in Japanese gardens is *niwaki*, which the Japanese themselves are perfectly happy with, as it instantly declares the purpose of the tree while leaving any specifics open to the imagination or further description.

Within the generic term *niwaki* are more descriptive names and styles. The suffixes *zukuri* or *shitate* refer to a shape, a style, or a procedure carried out on the tree. Trunks can be described as bendy (*kyokukanshitate*), straight (*chokukanshitate*), twins (*sokanshitate*) or (literally) lots (*takanshitate*). The shape of foliage on branches can be described as balls (*tamazukuri*), steps (*danzukuri*) or shells (*kaizukuri*, *kai* being a cockle), although a certain degree of imagination is sometimes needed. Trees with one branch stretching out sideways are described as one-sided branch (*katanagareshitate*), while an irregular branch or trunk could be described as meandering (*nagareedashitate*).

None of these terms pushes the lexical boat out too far, and

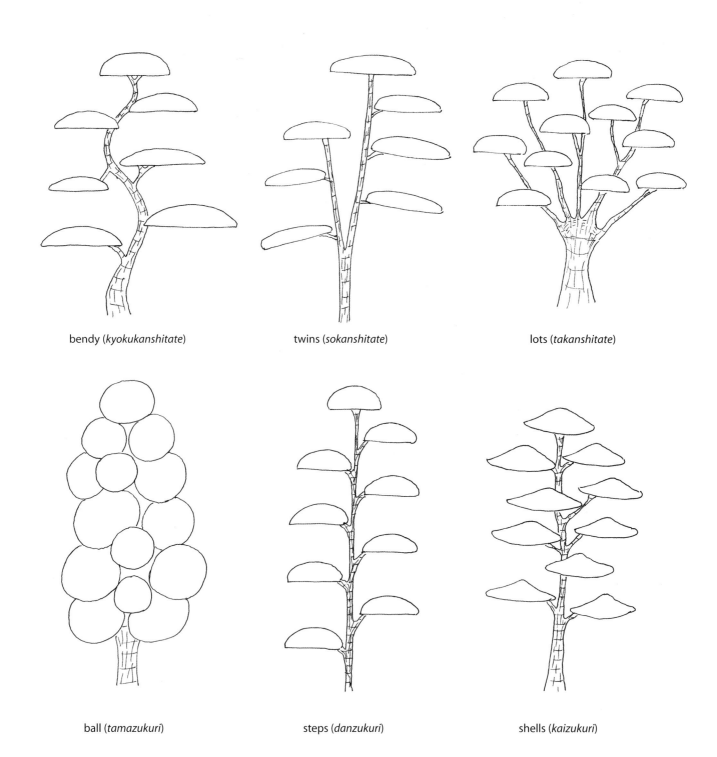

bendy (*kyokukanshitate*)

twins (*sokanshitate*)

lots (*takanshitate*)

ball (*tamazukuri*)

steps (*danzukuri*)

shells (*kaizukuri*)

Different pruning styles are given descriptive names.

most gardeners would simply refer to a tree having a good shape (*ii kanji*). Though it may be fun, and occasionally useful, to use descriptive terms (and let's face it, we all like a bit of classification) I would urge you not to get too concerned with pedantic issues of style, and concentrate instead on simply making the tree look good.

Above: *Juniperus chinensis* '*Kaizuka*' in the *tamazukuri* style, at a nursery in Osaka Prefecture.

Right: The flattened branches of this *Podocarpus macrophyllus* specimen could be in the *kaizukuri* style. Jizo-in, Kyoto.

Right: An example of *fusezukuri*: *Pinus densiflora* trained over a bamboo framework. Imperial palace, Kyoto.

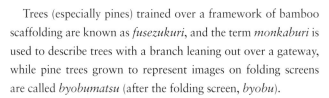

Trees (especially pines) trained over a framework of bamboo scaffolding are known as *fusezukuri*, and the term *monkaburi* is used to describe trees with a branch leaning out over a gateway, while pine trees grown to represent images on folding screens are called *byobumatsu* (after the folding screen, *byobu*).

Concerning the naming of trees, Japanese gardeners and landscape designers use the common Japanese name rather than botanical names. As with English common names, these are often descriptive, such as the black pine, *kuromatsu* (*Pinus thunbergii*), with its dark, almost black bark; the red pine, *akamatsu* (*P. densiflora*), with reddish bark like that of *P. sylvestris*; and the five-needled pine, *goyomatsu* (*P. parviflora*). Non-natives often have adopted names, such as *himarayasugi* (*Cedrus deodara*, the Himalayan cedar). Newer introductions tend to have adapted versions of the botanical or Western common name, so *Eucalyptus* species are known as *yukari*, and *Olea europa* as *oribu* (in both cases, the closest Japanese phonetics gets to English).

As you would expect, pruning techniques have various different names, too. The clipping of shrubs, usually evergreen azaleas, is known as *karikomi*. Pine trees are pruned in two ways, *midoritsumi* (literally, 'picking green') involves the

Monkaburi: *Pinus thunbergii* trained over a gateway in the suburbs. Osaka Prefecture.

Above: *Karikomi*, clipped evergreen azaleas. Private garden in Kyoto.

Right: Entrances to temples can be open or (below) more enclosed.

pinching out of new growth in early summer, followed by *momiage* (which translates, strangely, as 'sideburns') during the autumn clean-up. Thinning, to preserve the natural habit of the branches and foliage, is known as *chirashi*, while at the nursery *fukinaoshi* is a technique for cutting back overgrown trees, creating a new shape. All these curious-sounding styles are discussed in relevant chapters throughout the book.

Niwaki in Temple Gardens

Temple gardens cover an extraordinarily wide range of styles, from grand strolling gardens to simple courtyards. Typically they are built around the various buildings that make up a temple, and sometimes even the approach from the street. Some temples have grand, open approaches, while others opt for a more enclosed, leafy atmosphere. Often there are several separate gardens belonging to one temple, built on different aspects, attached to different buildings. These gardens are viewed in one of two ways. From within the buildings, usually on the veranda (called *engawa*), the garden is designed to be visible from sitting height. Chairs are not used in traditional Japanese rooms, so the viewer sits cross-legged, or kneels. From this position the garden is framed by the wooden architecture of the building, every point in the room creating a different picture.

These gardens, whether the minimalistic, raked gravel *kare-sansui* gardens such as Ryoan-ji, or the more heavily planted gardens, always depict some sort of landscape, ranging from the abstract to the literal, and can incorporate all the elements of the Japanese garden: rocks, gravel, water, lanterns, bridges,

pagodas, and, of course, trees. The trees are used on a scale that reflects the landscape itself, and therefore range from as small as waist height (to imply a vast landscape, dotted with trees) up to enormous individual specimens (in a smaller-scale setting).

Komyo-ji, hidden away in the outskirts of Kyoto, is a good example of a temple with a garden designed to be viewed from the veranda. The flat, enclosed area of raked gravel is scattered with rocks, symbolizing islands out at sea. To the left of the view is a steep slope, planted with *karikomi* and an impressive rock formation. The back of the gravel area is bordered by a wall capped with tiles, in the centre of which is a colossal gateway. Finally, to the right is a pine standing in an area of moss. The pine is tall, larger than would normally used in such a garden, but its size is intended to balance out the mass of the gateway. One lower branch is trained out over the gravel, linking the height of the tree with the flat expanse of the imagined landscape. This branch seems separated from the tree itself, and occupies a far less defined scale so that the visitor is compelled to ask: Is it a part of the metaphysical landscape of the raked gravel and rocks, or merely the lower branch of a pine tree?

Above: **Viewing the garden from the** *engawa.* **Raikyu-ji, Takahashi.**

Right: **Komyo-ji, Kyoto.**

Below right: **The grounds of Komyo-ji, perhaps two weeks too early for the maples.**

The grounds of Komyo-ji are famous for their maples, and are open all year round, but the garden itself is open to the public only in November, when the maples are at their best. I learned this the hard way, turning up in late October before the maples were in their prime. At first I was not allowed in, but with a fair bit of pleading, playing my *gaijin* wild card, I was eventually allowed a quick peek. (The term *gaijin* is used for all foreigners, and, as visitors to any foreign country know, a combination of innocence and ignorance, authentic or otherwise, can get you a long way.)

Other gardens are designed to be walked through, as well as (or instead of) being looked at. Toji-in, also in Kyoto, is one such example. From the verandas of the temple building certain views are available, but step out into the garden and these views change with every step. Visitors take their shoes off in temples (as in all Japanese homes), leaving them at the entrance in return for a pair of slippers. When it comes to walking into the garden, outdoor, slip-on shoes are available. One size fits all (or not, if, like me you have large, Western feet).

Making your way around Toji-in, trees and clipped *kariko-mi* move in and out of view, and trunks and branches appear beside the path, unseen from the veranda. The path guides you around a pond, up a slope via a small tea house, and then further away from the buildings to a second, less formal pond. *Ilex integra*, which from the temple building looks more like a bushy shrub, transpires to be grown in the remarkable *daimochi* style, with an enormously squat trunk, lurking by

Above: **Toji-in, Kyoto.**

Right: **The tea house at Toji-in.**

Below right: **Irises and grasses give the second pond a less formal look at Toji-in.**

the path. The changing levels along the path reveal new relationships among the clipped azaleas—and with this, new reflections in the pond.

There is a lovely balance of clipped shapes and pruned trees, softened with grasses, around the pond. Toji-in is well worth a visit any time of year, and in fact was my mother's favourite garden in Kyoto when she visited. (Beware: there is another, more famous To-ji in Kyoto, with an interesting monthly market, but from the gardener's point of view it is less significant. Taxi drivers, on the other hand, seem to prefer it.)

A feature many temple gardens share is the backdrop of hillside. For example, Kyoto is bordered by hills to the north, east and west, and many of the temples are nestled into these slopes on the edge of town. A typical design sees the garden backing into the slope behind, heavily planted with cryptomerias, maples or bamboo. When there is no hill, one is often manmade, or implied through planting. The level to which these backdrops are incorporated into the garden varies; trees can be pruned as garden trees, or raised and thinned, opening up the woods behind, creating shadows and a sense of depth. Regardless of the level of intervention, these hills link the garden into a wider context, bringing with them elements of nature—the screech of cicadas and the scent of flowering trees in the summer; autumn colour, leaf drop and then the spring flush of new growth.

Some gardens link the hillside backdrops into their design by using similar planting in the foreground, connecting the hills with the garden. Ritsurin-koen in Shikoku, and the Adachi Art Museum in Shimane Prefecture (although not temples, and both far larger than most gardens in Kyoto) are heavily planted with pines, echoing the natural planting behind.

The size of the garden pines is cleverly controlled to blur the division between garden and backdrop, merging the two and expanding the scale of the garden considerably. When actual views are incorporated into the garden, this is known as *shakkei*, or borrowed scenery. There are some famous examples of this, often involving Mount Hiei in the background. This is a prominent hill to the northeast of Kyoto, visible from many of the temples in the northwest hills such as Shoden-ji.

Above: The backdrop of the hill is an integral part of the garden. Chishaku-in, Kyoto.

Above: The hills in the distance are incorporated into the garden through the repeated use of pines. Adachi Art Museum, Shimane Prefecture.

Below: The informal atmosphere of a *roji* garden. Zuigan-ji, Tokushima.

Niwaki in Tea Gardens

Tea gardens, although easily recognizable, are perhaps the least typical of Japanese gardens. They often appear within temple gardens, but there are no impressive rock formations, ponds or raked gravel, and the scale is usually small and personal. Here, the garden is no more than a simple path from the main building to a small tearoom; sometimes it is not even clear that it is a garden at all, so simple and informal is the atmosphere. Known as *roji*, literally meaning 'dewy path', the garden's function is to prepare participants for the tea ceremony ahead—to relax them, allowing them to forget the outside world, focusing instead on the inner self, almost in a meditative way. Modest and understated, the planting is less formal than in temple gardens, with shady, damp, mossy places, more like woodland than garden. The trees are often thinned rather than clipped, creating a lighter, more natural feel. Paths and plants are damped down for guests, especially in the heat of summer, provoking the cool, damp smells of nature and the sparkle of wet leaves.

The range of trees used in the tea gardens differs slightly from that of other gardens. Shade-tolerant woodland plants are favoured over pines, and evergreens such as *Podocarpus macrophyllus*, *Quercus acuta* and *Q. glauca*, *Camellia japonica*, *Fatsia japonica* and *Aucuba japonica* are common. Maples, of course, feature strongly, as they are ideally suited to the semi-woodland environment created. Nothing as showy as flowering cherries is used, but the more solemn figure of *Prunus mume* is sometimes included to provide seasonal interest.

The subtleties of the outline and texture of trunks are focused on; trees can be raised (their lower branches removed)

Trees such as *Podocarpus macrophyllus* are often thinned, rather than clipped, in tea gardens.

Above: The natural simplicty of the tea garden. Shinyodo Sanso, Kyoto.
(Photo by Edzard Teubert)

Below: The essence of woodland is universal. West Sussex, England.

to enhance the meandering line of the trunk. Overhead, the branchwork and shape of the trunks is paid careful attention. Constant pruning, taking out central leaders and straight growth, in time creates the spidery zigzag patterns in branches that so define these gardens. Whereas shears are normally used to clip trees such as *Podocarpus macrophyllus*, this would create too bold and strong a shape in the tea garden, so the new growth is thinned out using a type of garden scissor known as *uekibasami*. This thinning results in a subtle effect, and it is often not immediately obvious that it is intentional, such is the atmosphere of the whole garden.

Shrubs such as *Fatsia japonica* and *Aucuba japonica*, so familiar to gardeners in the West, are treated differently from how we might expect. Rather than being cut back into dense bushy shapes, they are raised up on one or two trunks, thinned to accentuate the graceful lines. All but the freshest foliage is removed. Tea gardens, like most Japanese gardens in general, tend to have simple groundcover, usually moss or bare earth; they are small, confined spaces, enclosed by walls of dull earthy colours or fences of natural materials such as bamboo. These surroundings accentuate the simplicity of the planting, which would otherwise be lost in larger, less defined surroundings.

The inspiration for this style of garden is primeval. One's senses pick up the same signals in woodland all over the world: the stillness, the smells and the light. Take a walk in any woodland, in a receptive mood, and the inspiration is waiting for you. Among the chalky South Downs of Sussex in England, beech trees (*Fagus sylvatica*) and ash (*Fraxinus excelsior*) are the dominant species, with yew (*Taxus baccata*) and box (*Buxus sempervirens*) growing in the shade below. Young trees send up spindly trunks, reaching for the light. Old specimens

of beech retain one or two low branches, spread horizontally by the lack of light, their foliage floating like ethereal swathes of mist hanging in the air. The evergreens, tolerant of the low light, slowly turn from straggly bushes into small trees. Signs of man's influence are everywhere; old pollards, long neglected, now form colossal trees, and areas of hazel coppice in different stages of regeneration demonstrate trees' willingness to be cut back hard. Every region's native woodland is slightly different, but the fundamental essence is the same, and it is this essence, this quiddity that tea gardens attempt to capture.

For foreigners in Japan, tea gardens are some of the most difficult gardens to visit. The most famous—Urasenke, Omotosenke and Mushanokoujisenke in Kyoto—are all part of the Senke tea school, and not open to the public. Some temples that open to the public, such as Kodai-ji and Keishun-in, both in Kyoto, have tea gardens within their grounds.

Byobumatsu. Ritsurin-koen, Takamatsu.

Niwaki in Public Gardens, Parks and Palaces

Broadly speaking, these gardens can be defined by their scale. Public parks such as Ritsurin-koen, castle gardens (most famously Nijo-jo in Kyoto), and the Imperial palaces in Kyoto and Tokyo, are all larger than most temple gardens. Typically they are strolling gardens, centred around a pond and designed to be seen from a certain route, as well as occasionally from the pond itself during boating trips.

Ritsurin-koen, in Takamatsu on the island of Shikoku, is one of the most fantastic gardens in all of Japan—especially for pine enthusiasts. It was originally built as a private garden, but during the Meiji Restoration (the return of power to the Emperor Meiji from the Shoguns, 1868–1912) it was turned into a public park. It covers an enormous area, and includes bridges, tearooms, six ponds, thirteen artificial hills, and open areas of grass like in a Western park. It is the pines, however, that make this garden exceptional—they are everywhere you look, clustered together on islands, scrambling up slopes, forming long, caterpillar-like hedges, framing views and leaning out over the ponds.

Ritsurin-koen features various styles of pines that are rarely seen elsewhere, as well as some trees considered to be the definitive examples of certain styles. The term *byobumatsu* comes from the folding screens (*byobu*) that are so often decorated with images of old, twisted pines. Cracked and chequered bark (particularly that of *Pinus thunbergii*) is often portrayed in these screens, usually as part of a series including seasonal trees such as maples and flowering cherry. This stylized, almost caricaturized image of the pine has in turn come to influence real trees, whose trunk and branches are trained to resemble the shapes that the screen artists present. It is a fascinating example of the cycle of inspiration that involves both art and nature, as human beings are inspired by nature and then in turn inspire others to re-create it. At Ritsurin-koen some of these *byobumatsu* are no taller than 1.8 m (6 ft.), covering hillsides to give the impression of an entire mountain of trees.

Elsewhere, pines are grown into enormous hedges, in a style known as *hakomatsu* (box pines). Viewed by looking down from the raised viewpoints of the undulating hills around the garden, these hedges resemble strange creatures—like enormous furry caterpillars—especially in late summer before they are given their autumn prune. From close up, it becomes clear that these are more than just hedges, grown to a certain height and then pruned back each year; they continue where the *byobumatsu* style has left off. Each tree is a maze of twisted, gnarled trunks, trained into the framework of the hedge. As you walk along the paths they flank, the dark, sinewy trunks are like creepers deep in the jungle, growing in an apparently random, chaotic manner. In one corner of Ritsurin-koen is a nursery area dedicated to the production of replacements for these hedges. Young pines in various stages are kept at the ready to fill any gaps that appear. It is fascinating to compare these pines in their formative stages with the finished, mature trees.

There are said to be so many pine trees at Ritsurin-koen that the rules about seasonal pruning are broken out of necessity. Instead, important trees in the main views are pruned at the traditional times of early summer and autumn, while the remaining trees are given attention in turn, on a regular cycle but not necessarily at the most appropriate time of year. The gardeners, working full-time, prune throughout the entire year.

Hakomatsu seen from the outside (left) and from the inside (below left). Ritsurin-koen.

Above: **Pine pruning on one of the islands. Ritsurin-koen.**

Above: **An enormous example of *Pinus parviflora*, beyond the pond. Ritsurin-koen.**

On my visit in September, a small flotilla of boats had crossed over to one of the islands, where the population of *Pinus densiflora* was being dealt with. Nets and booms were rigged along the banks to keep the water clean from fallen needles. I asked one of the gardeners how often they pruned the pines, and his answer confirmed what I had heard: "*Mainichi*" ('every day').

Individual trees manage somehow to stand out from this amazing collection at Ritsurin-koen. A tremendous specimen of *Pinus parviflora* in front of the tea house (best viewed from across the pond) started life as a *bonsai*, grafted onto the rootstock of the more vigorous *Pinus thunbergii*, as is common practice in *bonsai*. Released from its tiny pot, and given the free rein of the ground as well as the extra energy of the rootstock, this tree had grown to be enormous—certainly the largest of its type that I have seen.

Above: *Hakozukuri*. Ritsurin-koen.

It is not just pines that impress at Ritsurin-koen, however. Much reproduced as an image is the view of the clipped *Buxus macrophylla* in the unusual form known as *hakozukuri* or box pruning. (This is the same name given to the box pines.) The art of clipping and *karikomi* generally involves rounded, organic shapes rather than these more abstract forms that seem to have more in common with a Cézanne landscape than anything else.

Niwaki in Private Gardens

Private gardens come in all shapes and sizes, from the grandest Kyoto residences to poky Tokyo courtyards, and from wealthy farmers' estates to rural back yards. The finest private gardens can be every bit as impressive as any temple garden, although the austere influences of Zen are less apparent, and the scale is usually smaller. Most homes, however, are in busy suburbs where the space allocated for gardens is small. Here you can witness some fascinating gardens, parts of which are visible from the road. To the front of the house, the garden is effectively a large screen, normally made up of large, clipped evergreen trees planted close together. They loom over walls, offering tantalizing glimpses through to the house.

Private gardens come in all shapes and sizes, from this farmhouse in Shikoku (above right) to a jungle of breezeblocks and overhead cables in Kyoto (right).

Above: Organically clipped *Juniperus chinensis* **'Kaizuka' and tall** *daisugi***-style** *Cryptomeria japonica* **in smart suburbs. Osaka Prefecture.**

Below: Various trees, including *Podocarpus macrophyllus* **and** *Cedrus deodara***, screening a large garden in Shikoku.**

Above: *Juniperus chinensis* **'Kaizuka' as a semi-permeable screen. Osaka Prefecture.**

Below: *Monkaburi, Pinus thunbergii***. Osaka Prefecture.**

Sometimes trees are grown to act—in a very Japanese way—as a semi-permeable hedge. Typically, *Juniperus chinensis* 'Kaizuka' or, in Kyoto, *Cryptomeria japonica* are thinned and clipped to such an extent that the hedge is implied rather than real. Perhaps because they live in such close proximity, the Japanese people are incredibly tolerant, patient and polite. They seem to have developed an implied respect for each other's privacy, whereby although nosy neighbours can look through into the house, they choose not to do so out of respect—so the hedge need only be a token, a symbol. The half-revealed, fleeting glimpse that is created belongs to the same aesthetic as a *geisha* hiding her face behind a fan, or even the use of paper *shoji* in the doors and windows of traditional houses.

One feature common to many front gardens is a tree trained over the entranceway, known as *monkaburi* (literally, 'gate covering'). This is usually a pine (*Pinus thunbergii*, *P. densiflora*) or *Podocarpus macrophyllus*. Rather like roses may be trained over archways in cottage gardens, or fastigiate yews are allowed to merge above a gateway to the village church, these trees have a side branch that frames either a small gate or the driveway. As well as screening the view to the house and framing the entrance, this branch also creates a feeling of entering into privacy as you walk underneath, leaving the bustling outside world and entering the calm of the home, although in the countryside there is normally a dog barking at you at this point.

Back gardens are more landscaped, often including elements such as lanterns, water basins (*tsukubai*) and footpaths. The planting is often lighter and softer than at the front. Deciduous trees such as *Acer palmatum* and *Lagerstroemia indica*, flowering in late summer, are common. They shade the garden throughout the summer, but allow the winter sun in after leaf drop. Most of the principles of traditional gardens are applied, on a smaller scale.

Above: *Tsukubai* in late summer.

These gardens are known as *tsuboniwa* (referring to the old measurement of tsubo, approximately 3.3 m square [35 ft. square]) and as far as their form goes they owe more to the tea gardens than any other. They offer cool shade in the hot summers and provide relaxing views from inside the house, giving a sense of the house being in a dappled glade in the woods. *Tsuboniwa* became popular as domestic gardens for these practical reasons; they are more homely and personal than many temple gardens, and their smaller scale is more manageable.

When gardeners in the West build Japanese gardens, they usually use temple gardens as their model. This is reasonable when making show gardens for parks, such as the Japanese garden at London's Royal Botanic Gardens at Kew, but it would be more accurate (and sensible) for gardeners instead to glean their ideas from the *tsuboniwa*—the direct equivalent of the domestic garden. The scale is more manageable, and the planting more varied than in the temple gardens.

Niwaki in Contemporary Gardens

For visitors to Japan, the number of traditional temple and palace gardens open to the public is astonishing. Weeks and weeks could be spent in Kyoto alone, without even scratching the surface of what is on offer. Finding something a little more contemporary, however, can be difficult. The new private gardens and corporate spaces in which Japan's contemporary garden makers' work is to found tend to be inaccessible to the general public, let alone tourists. These gardens are elusive. In contrast to England, Japan has no Yellow Book system (where private gardens open to the public under the National Gardens

Glimpses of gardens: a formal, traditional courtyard in Kyoto (top) and a newer suburban one in Osaka, on a day when the gardeners were at work (above).

Scheme), and there are very few books on the subject. *The Modern Japanese Garden* (Freeman and Nose 2002) is, however, a brilliant book, featuring a wide range of gardens, with fantastic pictures and informative text.

Throughout the twentieth century Japan went through many political, economic and social changes. Most recently, the rise in the population has seen massive suburban spread, with countless new developments springing up around large towns. As an English teacher in the late 1990s, I lived in a town called Omiya. My daily walk to the station took me past a rice field, complete with its own population of frogs. Returning four years later, I got lost trying to find my way from the station to my old home; to my horror, the rice field had been turned into an apartment block. On the positive side, though, this new housing has been an important source of new gardens, and is redefining the traditional *tsuboniwa*.

Contemporary Japanese gardens can be traced back to the work of Mirei Shigemori, who created gardens in the 1940s through to the 1960s. He created some strikingly modern temple gardens, most famously at Tofuku-ji, in Kyoto. His trademark was moss-covered hillocks and bold rockwork, seen throughout garden history in Japan, but taken to a new, more abstract level by Shigemori. Drawing heavily on past traditions, he was also influenced by modernism, as can be seen in the chequered patterns of moss and clipped box at Tofuku-ji in Kyoto.

Many contemporary gardens for temples and private homes continue to be built in the traditional styles, giving no clues as to their age. Yet there have also been definite trends among garden makers, who are increasingly pushing out in new directions, using modern materials, and drawing upon influences from around the world.

The cost of making gardens in Japan is high. Individual rocks, valued not merely for their shape but also for their geological type and even their history, can cost a small fortune. Mature trees, trained and shaped by nurserymen, can be a hundred years old or more. All this, coupled with the high cost of labour in Japan, results in high prices, especially for larger projects.

Some say it is this high cost of labour that has helped to popularize a contemporary look. The dominant tree in traditional gardens has always been the pine, the maintenance of which is extremely time-consuming; individual trees can take two or three gardeners a whole day to prune, twice a year. Having more than one or two pines clearly adds to the bill, and by using other trees, which demand less time and effort, costs are kept lower. The trees that have become popular tend to be a mixture of broadleaved evergreens, such as oaks (especially *Quercus myrsinifolia*), hollies (such as *Ilex pedunculosa*) and *Castanopsis cuspidata*. Along with these evergreens, *Acer palmatum*, *Stewartia pseudo-camellia*, *Cornus kousa* and *Styrax japonica* are also frequently used. These trees are pruned and tended to each year, but the styles are typically more natural. They are often grown as multi-stemmed trees, and are thinned rather than clipped, to give a lighter and more natural feel.

This use of more naturally shaped trees creates a woodland atmosphere, with areas of dappled shade in the summer. Japanese summers are fantastically hot, and the cool, shady gardens offer respite from the heat. Perimeter hedges are usually tall evergreen affairs, thinned each year so as not to effect a feeling of complete enclosure. In fact, rather than being true hedges, they are really rows of closely planted trees serving the

Left and far left: Modernism at Tofuku-ji, Kyoto.

Right: Easily identifiable motifs at the Kyoto Garden, Holland Park, London.

purpose of a screen but doing so in a natural way, as if to suggest that over the wall lies woodland (not neighbours). The traditional *niwaki* are not ignored altogether, depending on the budget and scale of the project, but in the contemporary gardens there is less dependence on them.

Certain rules that seemed to underpin the traditional gardens often are ignored in these contemporary situations, especially when it comes to plant material. Where traditionally only a very limited range of plants was used, it is now common for individual garden makers to use a wider range. In fact, it is their very individuality that really defines recent generations of garden makers. Some adhere to the traditional use of native plants only, while others may welcome exotics, or a greater range of flowers.

Austere areas of raked gravel tend to be ignored, often replaced with decking or terracing. Here the traditional aesthetics still hold sway, and the techniques, materials and patterns still invoke the spirit of traditional gardens and Japanese design in general—even if an outdoor eating area has been incorporated into the design.

So although the underlying principles of the Japanese garden—such as the influence of the landscape, and the stylized representation of nature—still remain, the end product of today's Japanese garden making often appears to have much in common with a Western woodland garden. In keeping with the Japanese spirit of meticulousness, however, it is all carefully controlled to create the impression of woodland, rather than allowing the natural woodland to dominate. This is, after all, what defines all Japanese gardens, old or new—the search for the essence of the landscape.

Niwaki in Foreign Gardens

Japanese-style gardens outside Japan are a peculiar phenomenon—and, to me, they are a constant frustration. Living in England (and I am aware that North America seems to fare better in intelligent representations of Japanese gardens than England does), I am constantly upset by the state of affairs; the better-known gardens, designed at the start of the twentieth century (often by respected Japanese designers), focus on all the easily identifiable, tangible motifs. The result? Pleasant, attractive and utterly pointless gardens that belong in a theme park—yet people seem to like them.

What these gardens show more than anything is that apart from convincing designs and all the appropriate hard materials, what defines real Japanese gardens is their constant maintenance—and the moment a collection of maples and azaleas are handed over to traditional English gardeners, it is unsurprising that they do typically English things to them. Normally this involves doing very little. Tea houses, lanterns and pond layouts are all well and good, but you should not for one minute think that they make an authentic Japanese garden. My gripe? I wish the gardeners would prune the trees.

If you are seeking inspiration but cannot get to Japan, I recommend avoiding these Japanese-style gardens, and instead looking closer to home. Orchards and fruit growing techniques—and, in a more general sense, the natural landscape all around us—offer far more insight into *niwaki* than misconstrued relics from the past.

Of course, if an authentic Japanese garden is what you want, an interesting conundrum arises: when it comes to plant material, should you use traditional Japanese *niwaki* or adopt

Recently clipped *Phillyrea latifolia* **contrasting well with the surrounding shapes and textures.**

Phillyrea latifolia **being trained as a semi-permeable screen.**

the Japanese approach and use trees native to your own country? It all becomes rather academic at this point, missing out on the vital element of emotional response. Rather than prescribing one or the other, I invite you to ponder over a theoretical Japanese garden, built in my hometown of Chichester, in West Sussex. Here, box and yew are the native evergreens (so is holly, but not locally, on the South Downs chalk) while the holm oak (*Quercus ilex*), introduced from Europe in the sixteenth century, has been as good as adopted (locally, at least) as a native in the landscape. Along with beech and oak, the dominant deciduous species, and hazel growing in the under storey, these can all be trained and pruned. The spring blossom of blackthorn (*Prunus spinosa*) provides seasonal colour. Rolling hills, orchards, dappled woodland carpeted with wild flowers—sound familiar?

Applying a Japanese approach to gardening, as opposed to setting out to imitate a Japanese garden, is braver and more creative, and I find that the results are far more stimulating. Rather than being paint-by-numbers affairs cluttered with bridges, *koi* carp or fake herons, they are real, living places, assimilating influences instead of bowing to them. With the traditions of both topiary and woodland gardens, coupled with garden styles as apparently diverse as Capability Brown's eighteenth-century romantic interpretations of the English landscape and the North American prairie-style gardens, most Western gardeners are well-versed enough to embrace the organic sculptural qualities of *niwaki* (as well as other elements and motifs from Japanese gardens, if they wish) and incorporate them into a more general context, without getting bogged down in pedantic issues of authenticity.

When you are released from these shackles, the choice of

plant material is expanded, opening up new possibilities for old regulars. Plants we associate with being Japanese really look no more Japanese than many natives from elsewhere. It is what is done to the trees to make them look Japanese that yields distinctive results. Pines are just one example: most mature pines, growing in the open, tend to carry a Japanese air, and *Pinus thunbergii* (a Japanese native) looks no more Japanese than *P. radiata* (from California). It is not the pine that looks Japanese; it is the other way round. The Japanese people look at the pine, and admire certain qualities, which they attempt to reproduce in *niwaki*. The joy of *niwaki* is that their influences are not restricted solely to Japan, but wherever trees grow. All that is restricted is our attitude and response to them.

My own favourite tree for *niwaki* use happens to be the Mediterranean native *Phillyrea latifolia*, an evergreen with small, dark green leaves, which grows naturally in dry, sunny areas. I once came across a grove of them in the garrigue landscape of Provence, in the south of France, growing among *Quercus ilex* and *Viburnum tinus*. They were small, wizened little things there, but in wetter, milder climates they make fantastic wide-spreading trees, with a very distinct character which many Western gardeners would describe as Japanese— and which the Japanese would describe as essentially tree-like. A mature tree (quite a rare spectacle, unfortunately) evokes the shape and texture of broccoli, but they are slow growing and it takes a while before the character develops naturally. As *niwaki*, that character is there for the taking, lurking near the surface, in need of a bit of coaxing. *Phillyrea latifolia* is very responsive; it is tough as anything, and can be cut back hard, trained, and clipped into shape as well as any Japanese native.

Phillyrea latifolia **clipped in the** *tamazukuri* **style.**

Cupressus glabra **(from North America) standing sentinel outside a barn in England. Not very Japanese, but so what?**

Once the realization sinks in that *niwaki* can exist outside gardens and that they need not necessarily be native Japanese plants, a whole world of opportunities opens up. Bored with bay cones by the front door? Fed up with formal box topiary? You know the answer; keep on reading.

Bonsai: *Niwaki* in Pots?

The distinction between *bonsai* and *niwaki* could not be more clear-cut: one lives in a pot, the other in the ground—simple as that. It is actually the similarities that are more interesting to us, for the two have much in common. They share the basic premise of representing the spirit and essence of a wild tree, and they use similar techniques (and similar terminology to describe them). Clearly the scale is different, and *bonsai* demands a greater attention to detail, but the difference in size between a large *niwaki* and a small one is far greater than the difference between the largest *bonsai* and the smallest *niwaki*. (Even within the general term of *bonsai*, the scale varies; the smallest, *mame bonsai*, can be as tiny as 15 cm [6 in.].)

No, it misses the point to simply say that *bonsai* are smaller. Why are they smaller? Or: why are *niwaki* bigger? (And why do they come in different sizes anyway?) The scale of *niwaki* is determined by their role and position in the garden. It is restricted, on the one hand, by the natural size that trees reach, and by the practical considerations of planting and pruning. On the other hand, how small can a *niwaki* be? The smallest I have seen is *Cryptomeria japonica* (the species, not a cultivar) growing in the ground, pruned to reach no more than 24 cm (2 ft.). *Bonsai*, however, are limited by the practical

Above: *Bonsai* **live in pots.**

Below: **Ground-dwelling** *niwaki* **often end up in ornamental pots in non-Japanese nurseries, such as here at Architectural Plants in West Sussex, England.**

considerations of their pots. Whereas *niwaki* are a part of the garden, *bonsai* are isolated: they are the garden, and in the case of styles such as *saikai* they are entire landscapes within the pot.

In Japan, *bonsai* are rarely found in the garden as such, but rather on low-level display tables near the house. In the garden itself, *niwaki* are always planted directly in the ground. Outside Japan, the distinction is less clear, especially with the recent spate of imported *Ilex crenata* in ornamental pots. Are they *niwaki*, or *bonsai*? Does it matter? In some cases, yes, it does. The whole point of *niwaki* is that they describe a landscape, whether real or imagined, and trees simply do not grow in pots in the landscape. So in the case of Japanese-style gardens, if authenticity is a concern, using *niwaki* in pots is wrong.

In non-Japanese gardens, free from the constraints of authenticity, *niwaki* can actually look rather good in pots. Although there is a strong argument that in fact plants like this are happier in the ground, the tougher species, such as *Ilex crenata*, are as well suited to life in a pot as most plants—provided they are watered properly, fed occasionally, and pruned regularly (which not only keeps them in shape, but also prevents them from outgrowing their pots). Inevitably, though, growing plants in pots sets them on course for gradual demise, which can only be halted by planting them out in the ground, where they belong.

An old *Cinnamomum camphora* specimen at a nursery, after being cut back hard.

3
Principles and Techniques

A word of warning: if you ever hope to grow your own *niwaki*, this chapter is crucial. It may not be as pretty as the others, and at times it does get rather technical, but it covers a great deal of ground, and it is absolutely essential that you grasp these key points before moving on. That said, nothing beats first-hand experience, and some of the following instructions will only really make sense after many years of observation. Understanding how different trees respond to pruning, how their buds break from old wood when cut hard, how simple actions can have long-lasting effects—it takes a lifetime, and that is why it is so much fun.

When I first started thinking about *niwaki*, and why they look the way they do, I felt stuck. Remember that up to this point I had been primarily interested in sculpture and I had no experience whatsoever in gardening or tree care (which I cite as being a good thing, as I never felt blinkered, like a cart horse). These remarkable trees I saw everywhere baffled me, and only after many years of hard work, and the odd eureka moment, did things start to make sense.

With the advantage of hindsight, here are my three most crucial observations:

- For all the variations in Japanese gardens, most gardeners strive to coax out the same thing from their trees: the character of maturity.
- With only a few exceptions, this character is achieved through training and pruning branches to give the impression that they are larger and older than they actually are. Training involves giving branches the outstretched, horizontal lines that mature trees have, while

pruning increases the number of buds available, effectively scaling the tree down, condensing it while maintaining accurate proportions.

- When you stop to think about it, you probably already know much of what is discussed in this chapter; it just needs to be looked at in a different light.

The final point is the most important. It was not until I was safely back home that I noticed the similarities between *niwaki* and a lot of what goes on in typical English gardens. Apple trees (and other fruit trees), for example, are trained in various ways to maximize fruit yields, but the techniques used are almost identical to the basic training carried out on *niwaki*. The reasons for doing it are different, but interestingly, the way the trees respond is very similar.

One of the hormones in trees is called auxin, produced at the top of the tree in the leader. It moves down the tree, acting as a growth retardant, preventing side branches from competing with the leader. (In this way, the hormone helps the tree to grow as tall as possible, as any competition would slow the leader's growth.) By cutting the leader, the flow of auxin is restricted, giving the chance for side branches lower down to grow more vigorously. Dormant buds, known as adventitious buds, sprout from old wood for the same reason. Moreover, training side branches achieves similar results, as it reduces the supply of auxin within individual branches, forcing new energy further back up the branch. For the fruit grower, cutting the leader and training the side branches results in more fruit, and for ornamental growers it means more character—as well as more foliage to train and clip into shape.

What this means for you is that any experience in growing,

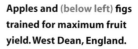

Apples and (below left) figs trained for maximum fruit yield. West Dean, England.

Below: An old coppiced ash (*Fraxinus excelsior*) in West Sussex, England.

training and pruning fruit trees can be transferred to *niwaki*—and if you have never dabbled in this area of gardening, chances are there is somewhere nearby where you can observe it. The gardens at West Dean, in West Sussex, are a constant reminder to me of how linked the pruning styles are, and in turn how obvious and universal many *niwaki* techniques are. Here trees are grown in all sorts of fantastic variations on the traditional cordons, espaliers and fans—best seen in the winter, when they are stripped down to skeletal form.

Other traditional Western skills are uncannily similar to Japanese ones; coppicing, pollarding, pleaching and hedge laying may be lost arts in the back gardens of the suburbs, but the basics of establishing and maintaining a hedge are fairly universal. Before you get carried away, though, cultivating *niwaki* is not as easy as that; technical skill is only half of it. Along with the cultural influences that underpin the cultivation of *niwaki*, and the technical skills themselves, there is another element to take into account: the Japanese idea of natural balance.

Natural Balance

Understanding the Japanese perception of natural balance is crucial to understanding *niwaki* in general. The idea refers to a sense of balance that arises organically. Tapping into this natural balance involves looking at how trees behave in the wild, the natural patterns of individual species in different situations—and accordingly, it is about embracing the imperfect, the asymmetrical and the irregular. However, cultivating *niwaki* involves not only observing nature, but also actively interpreting it; in Japanese culture and aesthetics it is this fusion between man and nature that is important, the building block for the garden. The way that human beings conceive of natural balance influences how they prune, shape and train their garden trees.

In the Japanese garden, odd numbers are favoured over even ones (trees are rarely planted in pairs, for example, but singly or in threes), asymmetrical balance is chosen over symmetry, and irregular lines are privileged over straight ones (although the naturally growing straight trunks of some conifers are encouraged). To this effect, trees with opposite branches are often thinned, taking out alternate branches even if this is not how

While the West may favour symmetry (a), Japan embraces asymmetry (b).

Right: Irregular shapes of *karikomi*. Anraku-ji, Kyoto.

Below right: Natural, organic forms contrast well with the geometry of architecture. Adachi Art Museum, Shimane Prefecture.

they would naturally grow. The clipped shapes of *karikomi* never achieve perfectly spherical shapes, like Western topiary attempts to do, but instead result in softer, more natural shapes. Geometry, only occasionally used in plantings, is usually reserved for buildings and hard landscaping, which accentuates even further the organic shapes and lines of the trees. The low, capped, courtyard walls, as well as the raked gravel, dark wooden uprights and white walls of temple architecture, create a stark backdrop to the natural irregularities of the plants.

Many people seem to intuitively grasp these aesthetics. Perhaps in each of us the capacity to appreciate and understand other cultures' aesthetics is built in automatically, but needs activating before we become aware of it. On my first trip to Japan it quickly struck me that here was something I had been missing, another piece of the jigsaw. This is not something that can really be conveyed without firsthand experience, and nothing can prepare you for the real thing.

Getting Started

Certain skills apply to every type and style of *niwaki*, so it is worth spending some time on this section before moving on to the individual trees. Some of these points are common horticultural knowledge, good practice regardless of what kind of pruning you are doing, while others are a bit more unusual.

First of all it is essential to understand, very basically, how trees and woody shrubs grow. Many people have the misconception that trees grow from the ground up, like toothpaste squeezed from a tube. Given more than a moment's thought, this obviously makes no sense. Think of the swing hanging from a low branch of an oak tree; it would end up out of reach if the tree were growing up from ground level. No, trees grow from the buds, at the ends of the branches and particularly from the top, so a branch that is 1.5 m (5 ft.) from the ground will stay at that height, as the tree grows taller. It is obvious when one thinks about it, and understanding it makes all the difference when training and pruning.

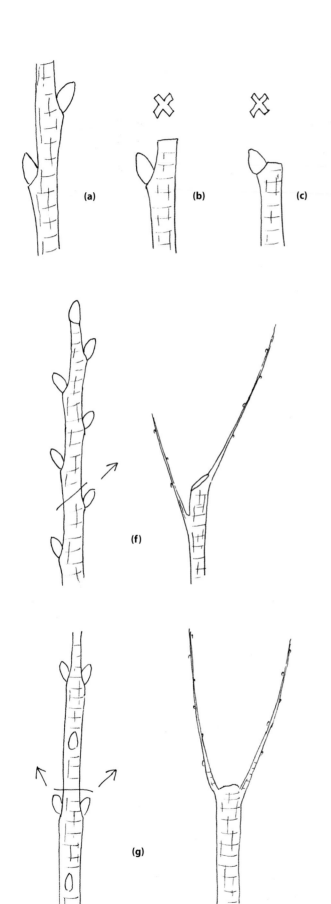

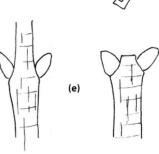

Tips for Cutting Branches

Most gardening books in the West, especially those with a section on pruning, instruct on the correct way to cut branches. This process is exactly the same in Japan, and it is important that it is done properly.

1   Always cut just above a bud. On alternate budding plants **(a)**, take care to cut neither too far above the bud **(b)**, nor too near it **(c)**. Instead, try to cut at an angle, sloping down away from the bud **(d)**.

2   On opposite budding plants you should make the cut straight **(e)**.

3   When cutting young branches, remember that the point at which you prune will determine the direction of the new growth. The last bud on the branch tends to be the dominant one, and normally you should encourage branches to grow outwards, or to fill spaces. Prune to an alternate bud **(f)** or set of opposite buds **(g)** to deliberately encourage growth in a certain direction.

4   When cutting branches back to the trunk, take care not to cut too deep. Cut just above the swelling under the branch where it meets the trunk (the bark collar) **(h)**. The aim is to minimize the circumference of the cut, to aid in the healing process. Do not cut too high up the branch, leaving a snag that will die back later.

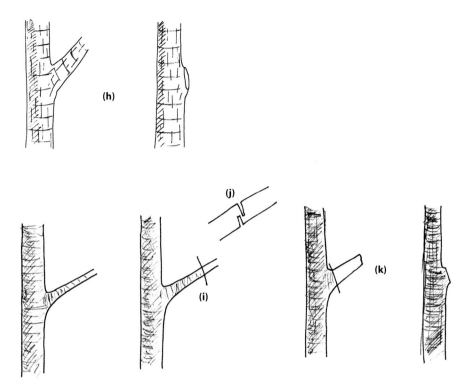

(h)

(j)

(i)

(k)

5 When cutting thicker branches with a pruning saw, remember that their weight can cause the branch to split before the cut is completed. Cut further along the branch than needed **(i)**, first making an undercut to relieve the pressure, then cutting from above **(j)**. Once the main length of branch has been removed, carefully cut off the stump **(k)**.

Fukinaoshi

The term *fukinaoshi* literally means 'to re-do'. It is the basic technique used to shape established trees, and involves cutting back to a framework of the trunk and main branches, before establishing a new shape. This technique of *niwaki* is used on various plants—*Ilex crenata* is perhaps the best known outside Japan, but others include *I. integra, Taxus cuspidata, Podocarpus macrophyllus, Quercus phillyreoides* (one of the many evergreen Japanese oaks) and *Camellia japonica*. Whether they are conifers or broadleaved, they are all characterized by their readiness to sprout from old wood when pruned hard.

Outside Japan, there is a huge range of plants that can be pruned *fukinaoshi*-style. The old topiary classics box, yew and holly can all be used, as well as most other species that respond well to topiary pruning, as long as they do not object to being pruned hard (so ×*Cupressocyparis leylandii*, fortunately, is out—as are *Cupressus* species, although they can be treated much the same as Chinese juniper in Chapter 6). *Phillyrea latifolia, Quercus ilex* (and any of the other smaller-leaved evergreen oaks such as *Q. coccifera*), *Euonymous japonicus, Myrtus* species (especially the South American *M. apiculata*), evergreen privet (*Ligustrum ovalifolium*) and even the larger-leaved *Ligustrum lucidum* are all suitable candidates.

A Google-generated translation of an online gardening forum (infojardin.net) describes *Myrtus apiculata* as having "much capacity to sprout again with force from his older parts". This peculiar translation actually sums up the prerequisites for *fukinaoshi* very well, admittedly with some artistic licence. At nurseries in Japan, enormous trees are sometimes dealt with according to this "capacity to sprout again with force". They might be trees salvaged from development sites or from old gardens being restored, and considered valuable enough for their size alone to restyle. The trunks of such trees

Fukinaoshi, a nursery practice, understandably not often seen in gardens.

Look closely at the tree. Is it single- or multi-trunked? Look at the branches and foliage: does the tree appear healthy? There is no point in using a dying specimen for a project like this. If it is a big tree, you may have to pull apart the branches and peer in. It could be that your tree is an old piece of topiary or part of a hedge, in which case the trunk and branches will be well developed, a perfect specimen to cut back hard.

For this exercise, we will presume that the tree has a single and roughly straight trunk, branches the whole way down to the ground, and suckers and epicormic growth (vigorous shoots growing from the base of the trunk). The first step is a thinning process, the aim being to remove all the unwanted branches to reveal the shape of the trunk and to make it easier to work on the remaining branches. Work slowly, but be confident. Understand right from the start that this sort of pruning will not harm the tree.

The Process of *Fukinaoshi*

To prune a tree in the *fukinaoshi* style, first remove all dead and broken branches, suckers and epicormic growth **(a)**. Then cut the trunk just above a set of side branches (at 1.8 m [6 ft.] in this example). Thin out the remaining branches **(b)**, trying to leave one every 15 cm (6 in.) or so, evenly spaced around the trunk. If the tree is in the ground, and has a front aspect, try to place more emphasis on the branches growing to each side, rather than to the front and back. Individual trees will have different branch patterns; some will make it very easy to create well-spaced sets of branches, while others will be more awkward, with large gaps between them—but this is inevitable, forming the individual shape of each tree. Finally, cut the remaining side branches back to about 30 cm (8 in.).

are often wrapped with hessian to protect the newly revealed bark from the elements, giving them an interesting sculptural quality. This kind of process is always completed at the nursery—never in the garden.

The main advantage of *fukinaoshi* over starting with a younger specimen is the benefit of many extra years' growth. When you cut back a larger tree to 3.6 m (12 ft.), instead of growing a young one up to the same height, the trunk is considerably fatter. This, in turn, gives the tree more character, making it look older and generally giving it better proportions.

The process of *fukinaoshi* can be applied to any size of tree, but for this exercise, imagine it is an old 2.4-m (8-ft.) *Ilex crenata* or *Buxus sempervirens*. From now on, think of it as a tree, its true size bearing no importance. The height will be reduced to approximately 1.8 m (6 ft.) during the pruning process. Start in spring, after the worst frosts are over.

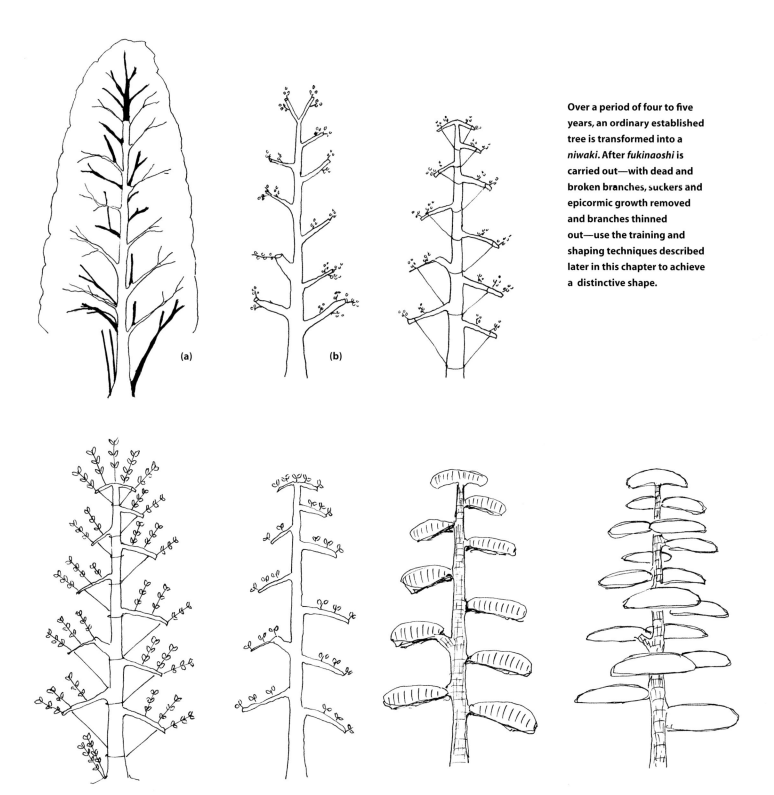

Over a period of four to five years, an ordinary established tree is transformed into a *niwaki*. After *fukinaoshi* is carried out—with dead and broken branches, suckers and epicormic growth removed and branches thinned out—use the training and shaping techniques described later in this chapter to achieve a distinctive shape.

(a)

(b)

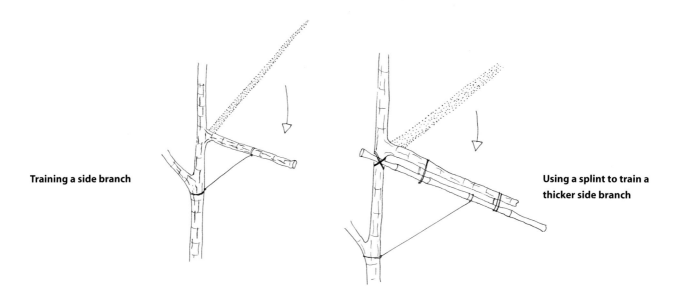

Training a side branch

Using a splint to train a thicker side branch

Depending on the individual plant, its type, age, and how it has been grown, there may be absolutely no leaves remaining now. Do not worry; the action of cutting back the branches will force the tree to send out new buds, known as adventitious buds, from the old wood, resulting in dense, bushy growth near to the trunk. Having stripped the tree down to a new framework, discarding the unnecessary clutter, the next step is to train the remaining side branches into place.

Training Side Branches

When growing *niwaki*, gardeners and nursery workers aim to make the tree look older than it actually is, to imbue it with a sense of maturity that young, naturally growing trees rarely have. Look around you at old specimens; most trees, given the space, spread out with age (fastigiate, columnar trees excepted). Pines are a fine example, their side branches often reaching out well below the horizontal. As they grow older, turning from mature to positively ancient, they start to lose branches altogether, creating the irregular, open look that characterizes old pines. Mature pines, silhouetted on a hilltop, demonstrate the importance of side branches better than any book can.

The process of training side branches to mimic those of mature trees is straightforward, and can usually be completed within a year. Use natural fibre string; in Japan they use *shuronawa*, dyed black palm fibre, but parcel string or garden twine are both fine, as this eventually rots down and does less damage to the bark. Note that the term 'branch' describes both the young side branches before they are trained, and the developed branches after shaping (sometimes referred to as clouds or pads). Check the flexibility of the branch, as some plants are more flexible than others, and can be affected by the season. In the spring and summer, when sap is flowing through the plant, branches are more supple, whereas in the autumn and winter, as the sap settles and the plant enters dormancy, the branches become less flexible.

Using the trunk as an anchor for the string, pull down the branch, hold it in position and tie tightly. The angle at which you tie the branch will affect the shape of the final result. Generally it should be 10 degrees below the horizontal, and lower still in some situations. Remember that by the time the branch has been shaped it will be larger and deeper, and we want the top to be roughly horizontal. Cut the branches back to encourage dense growth nearer the trunk. Depending on the size of the tree, the length of branches varies, and to allow light to the lower branches they should be slightly longer at the bottom (much as hedges are often cut wider at the bottom than the top). Typically for a small 1.8-m (6-ft.) *niwaki*, with a width of 90 cm (3 ft.), the branches should be cut to 30 cm (12 in.).

Some branches are too thick to train in this way, and will need splinting. Use a length of bamboo cane, tying the thick end to the branch at the trunk end. Notice how in the illustration the end of the cane sticks out beyond the trunk, to avoid gouging the bark. Tie the branch to the cane, and then train it down into position, tying as before.

Very thick branches will be too rigid to train at all. The solution is to cut them back, and train the resulting new growth instead. There are two options:

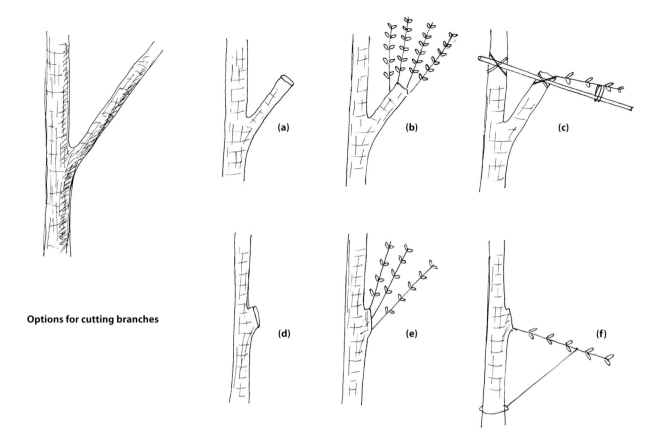

Options for cutting branches

(a)

(b)

(c)

(d)

(e)

(f)

1 Cut the branch back to 30 cm (12 in.) **(a)**. The following spring **(b)** thin the new growth down to one shoot and train down using a splint **(c)**. This adds a touch of variation and gives an interesting effect to the tree, having one or two branches that grow up before they are trained flat. Look at old trees, especially pines, and you will notice that they often have branches growing like this.

2 Alternatively, cut the branch completely, leaving a small stub **(d)**. When new growth is produced the following spring **(e)** thin this growth to one shoot, and train down **(f)** as shown.

Small branches will set within the year, but more stubborn ones will need longer. Every so often check the string, especially around the trunk, to make sure it is not cutting into the bark. Re-tie if necessary. Do not be afraid to change your mind, re-angling branches or removing them completely. *Niwaki* are works in progress all their lives, and it is never too late to make changes.

Right: A newly trained *Quercus phillyreoides* specimen.

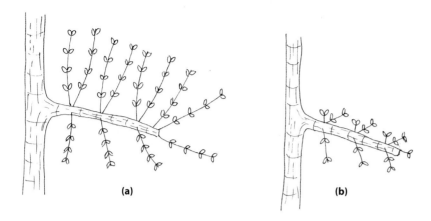

(a)

(b)

Consolidating Side Branches

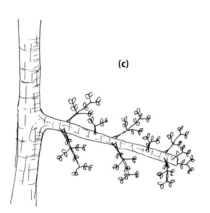

(c)

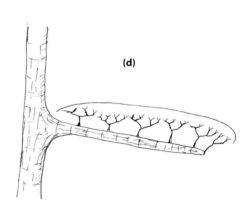

(d)

Consolidating Side Branches

In autumn, or the following spring, start working on the overall shape of the side branches. For all broadleaved trees, and some conifers, this is the same process, but the pines receive a different treatment, discussed in their own chapter.

1 To establish width to the branches, retain any new perpendicular growth, creating a paddle shape **(a)**. Decisions can be made about the overall shape of each branch at this point, cutting back this new growth to the desired length to create the overall surface area of each branch. Some styles of *niwaki* have very broad, flat branches, while others have far smaller, rounded ones. At the same time, cut back the new vertical growth to one or two buds, so the paddle shape is almost flat **(b)**. It will not look very promising at the moment, but you are laying the foundations for the future. (Cutting back to two buds allows a dense structure to form close to the original branch.)

2 Later in the summer, pinch out or cut back all new growth, again to one or two buds, to establish a good framework **(c)**.

3 Over the next two years regular trimmings will build up the branches. Start working on the shapes of these branches. They should be wide and gently sloping, low and flat **(d)**. For smaller-leaved trees, start using shears or long-bladed *hakaribasami* rather than secateurs. Do not be afraid of cutting through leaves with your shears; it does no harm, and is the only way to achieve smooth outlines.

The undersides of the branches are as important as the tops. Clip the bottoms so they are flat and sharp. As the tree develops, become more particular about clipping times; twice a year is the minimum—once in early summer after the first flush of growth, and then again in late summer. Depending on the growth of the tree, and your own commitment and levels of fastidiousness, you could clip every four weeks or so over the

Ilex crenata, ready for a tidy-up.

summer. You will find growth at the top is more vigorous than on the lower branches (the proper term is 'apical dominance'), and will need harder clipping to keep a good balance. Always look out for epicormic growth—it tends to spring from nowhere and messes up the outline of the trunk, but thankfully is easily removed.

Making the Head

Making the head is a vital skill to learn; it can be applied to a wide range of trees and styles. Although the plant type may vary, the basic technique is the same, essentially training three or four side branches into a flattened umbrella shape at the top of the tree.

1 Some trees will have a perfect set of side branches at just the right height **(a)** and these can be trained down to form the head in much the same way that side branches are developed in the preceding section. Cut the trunk just above these side branches **(b)** and go straight to the second step.

In other situations there might be no suitable side branches at the point you want the head **(c)** and you will have to cut the trunk to encourage new growth, which can be trained down the following year. The point at which you make the cut becomes the top of the 'neck' **(d)** so think carefully about how long you want this neck to be, in relation to the rest of the tree. Over the following summer new vigorous growth will spring from the cut leader. The next spring, thin it down to four shoots, regularly spaced around the leader (left, right, front and back) **(e)**.

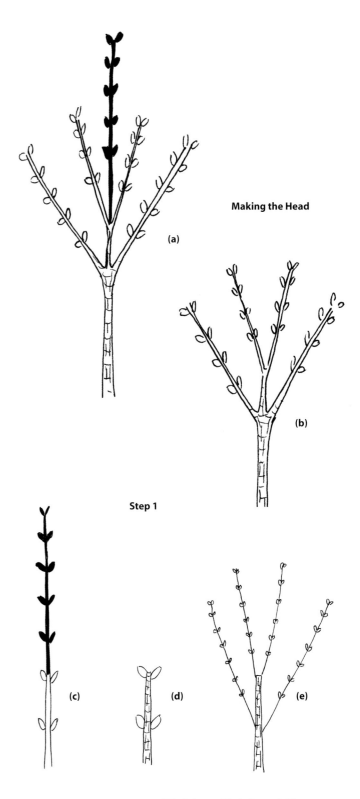

Making the Head

(a)

(b)

Step 1

(c)   **(d)**   **(e)**

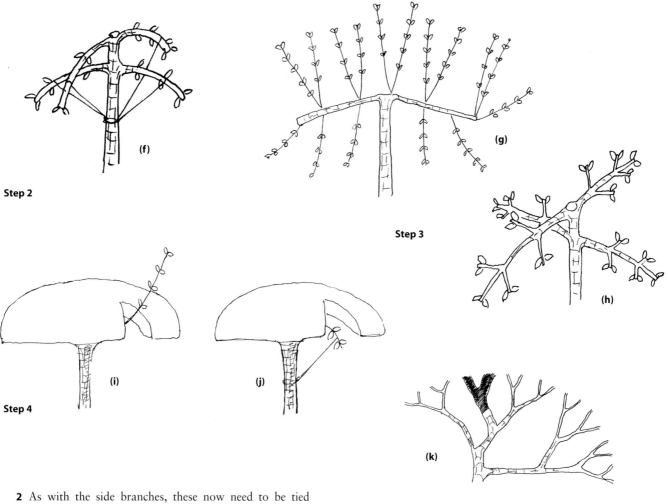

Step 2

Step 3

Step 4

(i)   (j)

(k)

Step 5

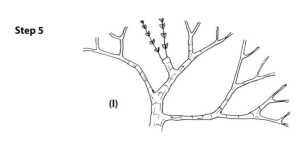

(l)

2 As with the side branches, these now need to be tied down, below the horizontal, using the trunk as an anchor point **(f)**. The width of the head is determined by how long these four side branches are. On a small tree of 1.8 m (6 ft.), cut them back to about 15 cm (6 in.) each, so the overall spread of the head is 30 cm (12 in.) Leave them longer if you want a wider head. The result, having tied them down and cut them to a uniform length, is that these side branches look rather like helicopter blades, or umbrella spokes.

3 Over the summer a mass of new growth will appear **(g)**. Depending on the growth rate of the plant (if you are working in a greenhouse or conservatory, or it is a particularly vigorous plant) you can continue work during this first summer, but normally it is worth leaving the plant alone completely until the following spring. The string should have done its job by now, and can be removed, although be prepared to re-tie if necessary. To develop the density of the head, cut back new growth to two buds all over **(h)**.

4 Over the next year or so, you may find areas in the head a bit bare or patchy **(i)**. Train down a new shoot into the gap; it will soon catch up and fill the space **(j)**.

5 After a few years of regular clipping, the growth in the head will start to become overgrown and woody. You will notice when clipping that the twigs near the tops of the branches are getting thicker and thicker **(k)**. These need to be cut out, about 2.5 cm (1 in.) or so below the level of foliage to allow soft new growth to develop **(l)**.

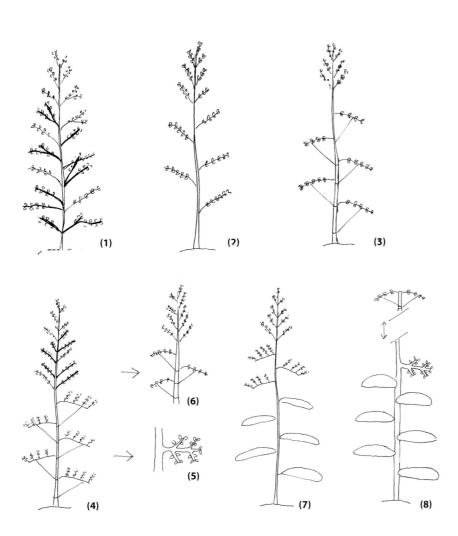

A young *Phillyrea latifolia.* England.

Starting from Scratch

Starting from Scratch

Not everyone has a bushy old box plant they are willing to experiment on, and the *fukinaoshi* process can seem daunting at first. Fortunately, a similar process can be used on younger plants—thinning and training each year, step by step.

1 Working from the bottom of the tree, select the branches you wish to keep. These should be regularly spaced around the trunk, but not directly opposite one another, ideally spaced every 15 cm (6 in.) or so up the trunk. (Leave the top 30 cm [12 in.] of growth untouched until the following year.)

2 Remove the unwanted branches.

3 Tie down the chosen ones, cutting them back to 20 cm (8 in.). Take care when pulling down these side branches—they are thin, and break easily, especially at the join with the trunk.

4 By the following year, the branches will have set, and you can remove the string. Most of the growth will have gone into the top of the plant, but some will have been directed into the side branches.

5 Leaving the new, horizontal sideways growth, cut back or train down the vertical growth to widen the area of the branch.

6 Next, look at the top of the tree. There should be enough material to work with from the previous year's growth, so continue from where you left off, clearing unwanted branches and tying down selected ones. Again, leave the newest growth at the top for the next year.

7 This process continues, gradually developing shape in the lower branches while all the time extending upwards.

8 When you have reached a good height, begin working on the head. Once the final height has been decided and the top

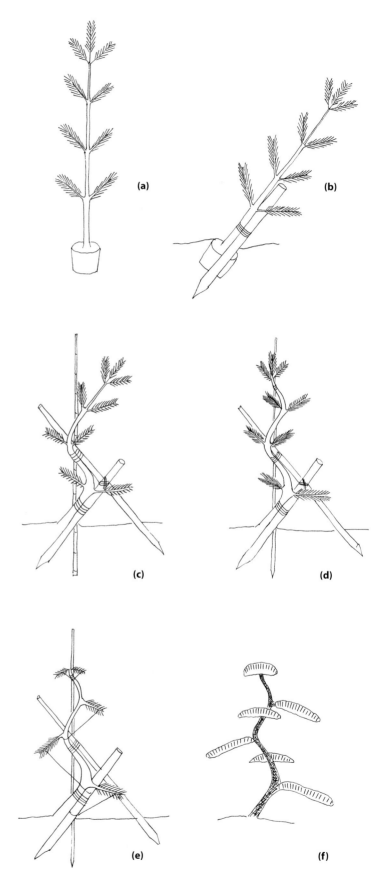

Bending the Trunk **(a)**

has been cut, side growth will be stronger than in the previous years, diverted further down the tree. With regular clipping the contours of the branches will quickly develop.

One advantage of starting from scratch is the flexibility of the young trees' trunks. This allows you more choice as far as the tree's overall shape is concerned, and these early stages are the best time to start introducing bends or kinks to the trunk. They might look contrived for the first couple of years, but as the trunk thickens up any changes you have made soon blend in.

Bending the Trunk

Pines in particular are often grown with a bend low down in the trunk. The scaly bark, especially that of *Pinus thunbergii*, adds great character. Start with a young tree, as it can be planted at an angle, giving the impression of having once been toppled by strong wind or of growing out from a steep bank.

1   Begin with a young pine **(a)**. Plant and stake at an angle of approximately 45 degrees (this might seem too much, but it is important to over-emphasize the bottom bend). To simplify the illustrations, there are no branches to the front or back of the trunk, but in reality these should be thinned and trained in the same manner **(b)**.

2   Using another stake, or stout pole, double the trunk back, and then add a third, upright pole near the base of the trunk **(c)**.

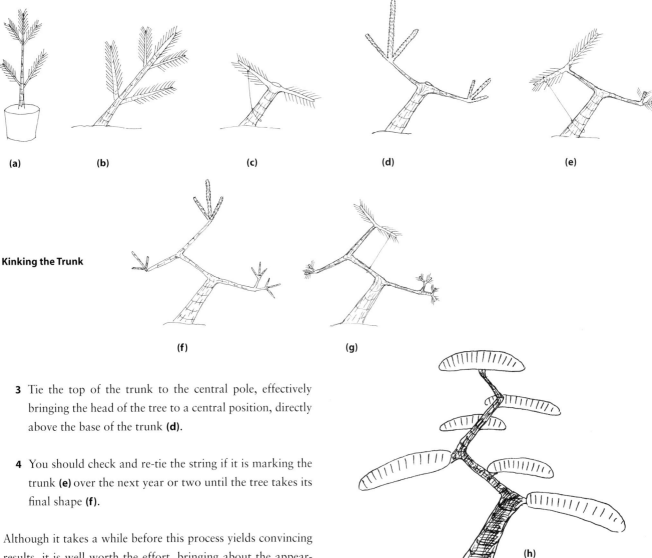

(a)   **(b)**   **(c)**   **(d)**   **(e)**

Kinking the Trunk

(f)   **(g)**

(h)

3 Tie the top of the trunk to the central pole, effectively bringing the head of the tree to a central position, directly above the base of the trunk **(d)**.

4 You should check and re-tie the string if it is marking the trunk **(e)** over the next year or two until the tree takes its final shape **(f)**.

Although it takes a while before this process yields convincing results, it is well worth the effort, bringing about the appearance of maturity that young, free-growing trees lack.

Kinking the Trunk

This achieves sharper, more angular results than bending the trunk. Again it is popular on pines, giving the impression that branches have been lost, perhaps in lightning strikes. Sometimes a single kink is all that is needed, but other times a series of kinks run up the trunk. For young pines it is an ideal way to introduce some character to the trunk, although to start with it can look harsh. Kinks can of course be combined with a bend in the trunk for even more character. The accompanying illustrations include pruning details for pines, but the kinking technique can be applied to any tree.

1 On a small pine **(a)**, planted at an angle **(b)**, cut out the leader, allowing the inward-facing branch to take over **(c)**.

2 The following year, repeat the process on the new leader, directing growth back towards the centre of the tree **(d, e)**.

3 This can be continued each year, working on the new flush of growth until you have reached the desired height. The head of the tree looks best if it is roughly central, in line with the base of the trunk **(f, g)**.

4 The result will look a bit contrived at first, but as the branches develop, the bark starts to show its character, and the trunk thickens, it will appear more natural **(h)**.

Training a young *Quercus ilex* specimen with irregular kinks. England.

Interesting branch structure could perhaps be revealed by raising or thinning **(a)**, the outline could be shaped into a bold silhouette with a pair of shears **(b)**, or individual branches could be accentuated using a combination of training and clipping **(c)**. Projects can be started in less than an hour, and then continued later in the year, defining and refining the new shape. Over the years the effect can be made to look more intentional, more Japanese, by thinning out superfluous branches and training others. If it all goes wrong, or you are not happy with the results, it will grow out pretty quickly and no one will be any wiser. Overgrown shrubs are prime candidates for this quick fix, and although the results might not appear entirely Japanese, they fit comfortably in general garden styles.

Finding photos that illustrate this is notoriously difficult. You need to have the right plant close at hand, preferably a year before you think of it, and you must be organized enough to take a photo before you start work, and then remember to take another when you have finished. Even then, the results never look as convincing as they do in real life, and illustrations get the point across far more effectively.

Wading In

As the name suggests, this is not specifically a Japanese technique, and for those of you obsessed with authenticity I suggest you move quietly on. It is, however, one of the most rewarding quick fixes known to the sculpturally inclined gardener, transforming shrubs and small trees from nondescript greenery to interesting, bold shapes almost instantly. It involves a fair amount of confidence (not to be confused with recklessness) and a certain vision. Angus White, at Architectural Plants, has coined the expression 'thrusting architecture' on plants, which sums it up pretty well.

Look closely at any plant, and it will suggest things.

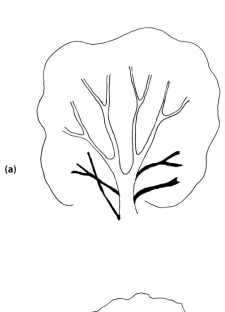

(a)

Five furious yet well-considered minutes with a pruning saw can reveal interesting branch structure.

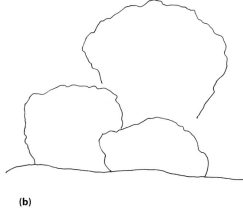
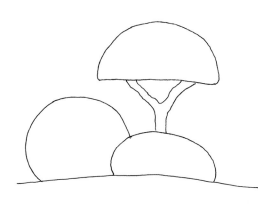

(b)

Overgrown shrubs can be transformed into bold, architectural outlines.

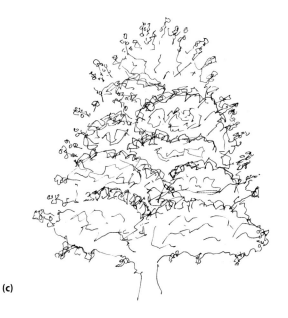
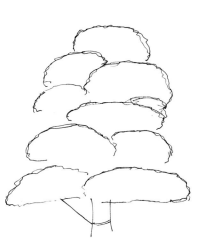

(c)

Look closely at larger shrubs and trees, and accentuate the natural spread of the branches with a combination of clipping, thinning and training.

The backdrop to a *kabuki*
stage. Uchiko, Shikoku.

4
Pines

The tree that single-handedly defines Japanese gardens is neither the flowering cherry, nor the maple, but the pine; no other tree holds quite such an elevated position in the Japanese consciousness. In Japan, pines seem to be everywhere, from the rocky coastlines and the deep mountains to the parks and gardens. Beyond their physical ubiquity, they are an integral part of Japanese culture, admired as much for symbolic reasons as for their physical qualities. They are a symbol of longevity, as they live to a great age and often appear to be older still, evoking wisdom and knowledge. They are resistant to change, remaining evergreen through the turning seasons, and they are strong against the elements—all virtues admired by the Japanese people.

An image of a pine forms the stage backdrop to traditional theatres, it adorns many a folding screen (*byobu*) and landscape painting, and poets praise the solitary pine for the emotions it stirs within them. In the New Year, cut branches of pine are used as decoration outside the house in a style known as *kadomatsu*, welcoming the gods into the home to ensure a successful year ahead. There is an expression *sho-chiku-bai*, meaning 'pine-bamboo-apricot', implying a ranking, the pine (*sho*) coming first, rather like a gold medal. This ranking is used in everyday life; for example, lunch boxes (*bento*) are rated at takeaway *bento* shops, with the tastiest, most luxurious lunch getting the *sho* rating. In one form or another, pines are everywhere you look.

That said, when asked what the pine meant to her as a Japanese person, my wife said nothing about the tree's symbolic value; instead, she recalled the terrible incident when a *matsumushi* (a big, hairy caterpillar that lives in pines) dropped into her hair as she played around a pine tree as a child. Not surprisingly, she has hated caterpillars ever since (but I suspect a certain amount of distrust is also reserved for the pine that caused the problem).

In the garden, the pine really defines what it means to be a *niwaki*. It is a native tree; different species (as we will see) grow in certain environments, which are reproduced in the garden. Loaded with cultural references, it is one of the most easily manipulated of all the garden trees, allowing the tree growers and gardeners to speed up the maturing process that gives pines so much character.

The three native species, *Pinus densiflora* (*akamatsu*), *P. thunbergii* (*kuromatsu*) and *P. parviflora* (*goyomatsu*), all have their own particular habitats. *Pinus densiflora* favours the hills and mountains, and is often planted in timber plantations in these areas. *Pinus parviflora* also grows in the hills, although it prefers a more sheltered environment. *Pinus thunbergii*, meanwhile, thrives on the windswept, rocky coastlines that surround Japan. When used in the garden there is often a direct physical or symbolic reference to these native habitats; the sea is evoked by rocks, gravel and ponds, while dense planting, undulating ground, rocks and waterfalls represent the mountains.

Generally *Pinus thunbergii* and *P. densiflora* are the more commonly used of the three; in smaller private gardens their roles are interchangeable, although traditionally *P. densiflora* was used more in gardens, and *P. thunbergii* was favoured in parks. *Pinus densiflora* is supposed to represent femininity, with softer, more luscious foliage and smooth bark, while *P. thunbergii* is considered a masculine tree, thanks to its rigid needles and rough, dark bark.

Pines are grown and trained into a wider range of styles

Above: *Pinus thunbergii*.
Raikyu-ji, Takahashi.

Below: *Pinus parviflora*.
Kinkaku-ji, Kyoto.

Above: *Pinus densiflora*.
Zenko-ji, Nagano. (Photo by
Jari Eikenaar)

Right: An interesting
relationship between the
curved trunks of two *Pinus
densiflora* specimens. Adachi
Art Museum, Shimane
Prefecture.

than any other tree. Trunks are often curved or kinked at an
early age, and limbs can be trained over gateways (*monk-aburi*), lanterns, waterfalls and ponds (*nageshinoeda*); in some
temple gardens, lower branches are trained out over areas of
gravel, or running parallel to path edges. Possibly the most
unusual pine I have seen was a specimen of *Pinus densiflora* in
a private garden I stumbled across while exploring Kyoto. The
tree had been trained to run along the top of the wall that
bounded the garden, and its one branch (or trunk, I could not

Above and below: This *Pinus densiflora* is trained along two walls of a private garden.

Above: An enormous old *Pinus densiflora* specimen trained out over a pond, contrasting well with the more naturally pruned trees of the same species behind. Zenko-ji, Nagano. (Photo by Jari Eikenaar)

Left: An interesting variation on *monkaburi*, with *Pinus thunbergii* trained almost as an awning. Osaka Prefecture.

Above and below: The outlines of pines can vary immensely.

Side branches can be splinted to bamboo canes (above), or cut back to create a zig-zag effect (below).

tell) ran 9 m (30 ft.) along one aspect before making a right angle bend and continuing for another 3 m (10 ft.). It acted as an extension of the wall, like a pleached hedge, and must have taken a good fifty years to train, perhaps edging forward 30 cm (1 ft.) per year.

The outlines of garden pines can vary immensely. Some are stronger, with more defined space between branches and denser foliage. Others are softer, with foliage heavily thinned and branches overlapping, resulting in a more subtle effect. Some trunks are straight, some bendy, and others decidedly kinked. Side branches too can be dead straight (splinted to bamboo canes), while others are constantly cut back throughout their lives to achieve a zigzag effect, particularly impressive when you look through the branches to a striking view beyond. Some trees are huge, as tall as you would expect to see them growing naturally (such as beside the castle walls at Nijo-jo), while some are no more than waist height.

Pinus parviflora stands apart from its cousins. Its needles are shorter and denser (they grow in fives, compared to twos

Above: *Pinus thunbergii*. Nijo-jo, Kyoto.

Above: Elongated branches of *Pinus parviflora* at a nursery. Osaka Prefecture.

Below: *Pinus densiflora* taking pride of place in a private garden. Kyoto.

Above and below: *Pinus thunbergii*. Imperial palace, Tokyo.

Above: *Pinus thunbergii* planted on rocky banks symbolizes the coasts of Japan. Nijo-jo, Kyoto.

for *P. thunbergii* and *P. densiflora*) and growth is slightly slower. This dense foliage is often preserved on the *niwaki*, with strong, tight branches that receive little or no thinning. Two styles are common: either rounded, flattened branches, or straight, elongated branches normally supported on poles. This latter style reflects more accurately the natural growth of the tree, which typically has long side branches, often curved up at the tips. Though less common than *P. thunbergii* or *P. densiflora*, specimens in temple gardens are inevitably highly impressive. There are interesting examples at Daisen-in and the grounds of Kinkaku-ji, both in Kyoto.

Most gardens have pines of some sort growing in them. Small private gardens might have just one, taking pride of place, usually visible from the house's main living room. Temple gardens often feature *Pinus thunbergii* in large numbers, planted on islands or around the banks of ponds, symbolizing the coasts of Japan. Other gardens, such as Ritsurin-koen, are packed so full of pines that they have become famous for their trees. The Imperial palace in Tokyo is another such example.

The garden at Adachi Art Museum. Shimane Prefecture.

Tricks of scale and perspective. Adachi Art Museum, Shimane Prefecture.

Outside the walls and moat of the palace is a park-like area planted with hundreds of *P. thunbergii*. The view is unlike that of any other garden in Japan, and well worth seeing; you can catch glimpses of it from the road, but it is more impressive when you look back at it, with Tokyo looming beyond.

One garden that must be mentioned when discussing pines is that of the Adachi Art Museum in Shimane, in the southern end of Honshu. This is a relatively new garden, built in the 1960s at the same time as the museum itself. It is one of the most impressive gardens in Japan, very well tended by a full-time team of six gardeners, full of pines and *karikomi* (see the following chapter), and displaying an extraordinary use of space and scale. The garden is viewed from within the museum, and from terraces at certain points around the museum buildings. In the foreground of the main view are large flat steppingstones that lead up to a pond, surrounded by enormous rocks and perfectly smooth, mushroom-shaped azaleas. Behind that, an area of undulating gravel rises up into artificial hills, dotted with pines. The gravel turns to grass, behind which are more pines and then a backdrop of natural hills.

What is remarkable about the Museum's garden is the incredible sense of scale it creates. Using such large rocks and *karikomi* to the front of the view brings the foreground right up to the viewer, making everything beyond it appear smaller and thus further away. The pines scattered among the gravel in the middle of the frame continue this trick of perspective: from the terrace they resemble large trees growing in undulating hills, although in reality they are no taller than 150 cm (5 ft.). The sense of scale is further stretched by continuing the planting of pines to the back of the garden, linking in with the hills beyond.

Which Pine?

The species of pine you choose is actually not as important as you might imagine. Issues of authenticity can arise if you are determined to create an entirely genuine Japanese garden, but in the true spirit of *niwaki* I recommend choosing a pine that you know grows well in your own region. In England, the native *Pinus sylvestris* grows virtually everywhere—and, being native, it fits the bill perfectly (although it is only truly native to Scotland). European natives such as *P. nigra* and *P. pinea* are both well known, and North American natives such as *P. aristata*, *P. contorta*, *P. radiata*, and *P. strobus* will all work fine, as will dozens more. The only species to avoid are those with very long needles, such as *P. coulteri* and *P. montezumae*, which tend to look messy however well trained and pruned they are.

Ultimately, your choice of species will affect the outcome in several ways. First, there is the speed of growth; *Pinus radiata*, especially growing somewhere cool and wet, will give you very quick results, but is more demanding in terms of pruning and maintenance than other, slower-growing pines. Then there is the colour of foliage; *Pinus parviflora* is relatively unusual in the Japanese garden in that it has greyer foliage than most other trees. Finally, there is the length, density, and number of needles; inevitably, species with longer, more numerous needles, packed closer together, will need more thinning to keep them looking presentable. Of course, there is no reason not to use the native Japanese pines, provided your soil is suitable (like many Japanese trees, *P. densiflora* prefers acidic soil). I merely urge you not to feel bound to authenticity, when the very nature of a *niwaki* lies in its native provenance.

Above: *Pinus sylvestris* makes a fine substitute for the native Japanese pines.

Right: A gardener at work on a *Pinus thunbergii* specimen, in the autumn *momiage* process. Special sleeves protect his wrists from the needles. Private garden, Osaka Prefecture.

The instructions provided here are general, referring to all appropriate pines. Pruning pines is different from pruning other trees; it is more complicated, the results take longer to achieve, and timing is crucial. Many people find the idea of pruning pines so alien they are afraid to even try, but in reality, although they look a bit different from other trees, pines behave in much the same way—so there is no need to feel intimidated.

A few basic principles in the early stages are relevant regardless of which style you choose; most of these principles relate to timing. Although pines respond well to pruning, like many conifers they will not re-sprout if you cut into the old wood; you cannot treat a pine like *Ilex crenata*, for example, and hack it back hard. Therefore, if you want to have a small pine in the garden, you must start young. Likewise, to achieve a bendy trunk, you will need to begin when the tree is still young and malleable, and if you are after dense branches close to the trunk, then this too must be started at an early age.

Basic Growth Patterns

The basic growth pattern of trees—how they grow from the tips of the buds, upwards and outwards—is never clearer than when looking at a young pine. Each year's growth is defined as a flush of side branches growing from the main (usually straight) trunk. The space between these flushes, the length of the trunk, represents how much the tree grew in that year. (You can discern the age of a young pine by counting the number of tiers; each one represents a year.) During the winter, when all growth has stopped, the top shoot on the trunk

demonstrates how much the tree grew during the last year, from the top set of side branches up to the tip. In late spring, the buds at the ends of all the branches, and at the tip of the top shoot, spring into life. Typically they will produce one leading shoot (known as the leader when it is the top of the tree) and four or more lateral, side shoots arranged evenly around the stem. At the top of the tree these four side shoots become that year's branches, but further down the tree, at tips of older side branches, the leading shoot continues to grow

Male strobili and one or two new buds. *Pinus densiflora.*

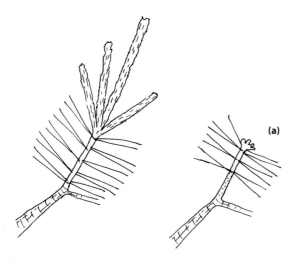

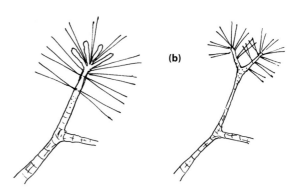

(a)

(b)

**Bud pinching (*midoritsumi*)
followed by thinning
(*momiage*).**

outwards, while the side shoots are arranged above, below, to the left and the right.

Pines are monoecious; they produce separate male and female flowers on the same tree, opening in late spring along with the new growth. (Technically speaking, conifers produce strobili, not flowers.) The male strobili, usually yellow, are the more conspicuous, especially when they release pollen in little clouds. They play no practical part in pruning, and can be ignored.

However, as far as we are concerned, the main difference between pines and most other trees is the way in which they respond to pruning. While broadleaved trees as well as some conifers (*Taxus* species being the most obvious) shoot from old wood when pruned, pines do not. Once the needles have dropped off a branch (needles usually last for two or three years, although on some species, notably *Pinus aristata*, they can persist for up to ten years or more) there is very little chance of provoking new growth.

Pruning randomly to a point on a branch that still has fresh needles does promote new growth, although the resulting buds tend to be close together, and need to be thinned out later on. This kind of cutting back is useful in early stages of pruning when you are establishing a framework, but ultimately the most satisfying and reliable way to guarantee new growth is to prune shoots that are less than one year old. In Japan, this is taken one step further: pruning (to achieve new growth) is only carried out on brand new shoots while they are growing in early summer. This technique is called *midoritsumi* (literally, 'green picking').

Midoritsumi involves pinching out all new buds (known as candles) to force a second flush of growth. On established trees, as buds start to grow they are pinched out by hand, right at the base **(a)**. Throughout the summer a second flush of growth appears, stunted by the late start. This flush is then treated with the process called *momiage* in the autumn, when it is thinned back to one or two of these new shoots, and old needles are pulled off **(b)**.

Bud pinching results in filthy hands. Pine resin (*matsuyani*) is sticky stuff—but if carried out at the right time, when the new growth has yet to open its needles and turn woody, it is easier than using scissors. The buds are soft, and should snap easily. If left for too long, they will need cutting, by which time it will be too late in the summer for a satisfactory second flush to emerge.

Different pine species, with different growth rates, respond to pruning in different ways. In Japan the buds of *Pinus thunbergii* (a faster-growing tree) are pinched out right at the base, whereas those of *P. densiflora* (slightly slower-growing) are pinched out up to 2.5 cm (1 in.) from the base, where regeneration will be quicker. Left unpruned, growth in one season is likely to measure up to 60 cm (2 ft.) for the leading bud, and as much as half that for the side growth. Following pruning, however, growth should be as little as 5–10 cm (2–4 in.), with up to five shoots. Nearer to the top of the tree, especially on younger, more vigorous trees, growth will be faster than on low side branches (as with most trees). This vigorous growth should be pruned more heavily, to achieve an overall balance.

Formative Pruning

Unless you are fortunate enough to inherit or buy an established tree, some basic formative pruning will be necessary regardless of which size of pine you begin working on. Formative pruning is best carried out in the autumn.

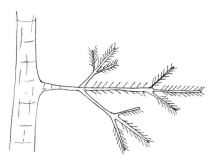
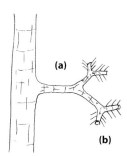

(a)

(b)

Step 1

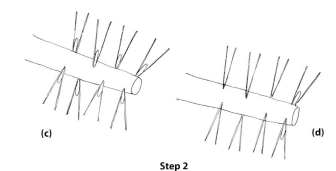

(c)

(d)

Step 2

Formative Pruning

1 Cut back the leading growth on each side branch to form a horizontal fork. If you want longer branches, cut back at the second set of side branches, but for shorter, denser ones, make the fork as close to the trunk as possible **(a)**. Follow the smaller side branches where you made this cut, and, if they too branch further down, cut out their leading growth **(b)** Then cut back the newest growth at the ends of the side branches by half to shorten the space between forks. (Being less than a year old, this new growth will regenerate easily.)

2 The next spring, as new buds develop **(c)**, thin them out leaving just two, growing in a V shape, facing outwards **(d)**. It is quite fiddly work, but the buds should break off easily at this stage.

3 The two remaining buds will develop into candles **(e)**. Pinch them back by half in early summer, before the new needles open **(f)**. The *midoritsumi* process now takes over.

4 That autumn, when growth has stopped, you can tidy up the tree with the *momiage* process. The short, dense growth that resulted from the early summer pruning **(g)** is thinned out, leaving two well-placed shoots in a V shape **(h)**. Old needles are picked off, leaving only the newest, freshest ones.

5 Over the following years, consolidate the density of the branches, gradually expanding outwards by pinching back the new growth by half each spring **(i, j, k)**.

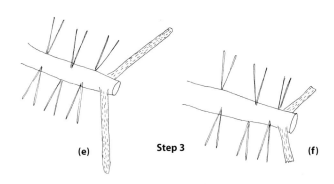

(e)

Step 3

(f)

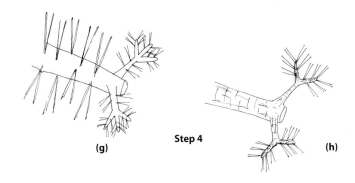

(g)

Step 4

(h)

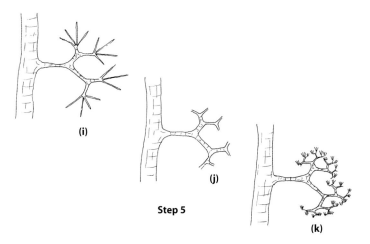

(i)

Step 5

(j)

(k)

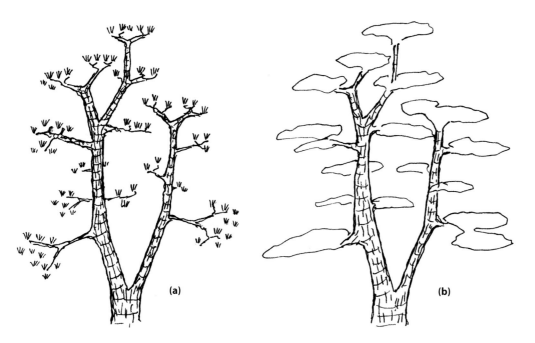

(a)

(b)

Thinning can be done in the autumn (a), or left until the following spring for a denser look (b).

Maintenance Pruning

As the desired spread of each branch is reached, pinch back the buds completely, rather than by half, to control the growth. Remember, timing is the key. Strike at the stage when the candles have extended, but before the needles have opened. Pruning earlier gives the second flush more time to develop, and the needles tend to be longer. Conversely, the resulting needles will be shorter if the tree is pruned later in the summer, which is sometimes done on smaller trees to balance the proportions.

The autumn thinning, *momiage*, is crucial once the framework has been established. It opens up the structure, allowing light in to lower branches, and prevents the growth from becoming too dense. The results can look overly severe for Western gardeners, and there is nothing to stop you from carrying out the tidy-up the following spring, before growth starts, if you prefer a slightly bushier look over the winter.

This *Pinus thunbergii* specimen was heavily thinned the preceding autumn. Now, in spring, the strobili and new buds are just emerging. Note how the branch structure and head have been developed.

Above left: *Pinus thunbergii* in late spring (May in Japan). The candles are half open, and the tree should be pruned in the next month or so.

Left: *Pinus densiflora*, having recently been pruned (*midoritsumi*) in early summer.

Below left: Another *Pinus densiflora* specimen, following the autumn thinning (*momiage*).

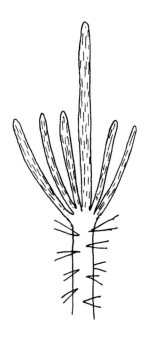
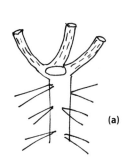
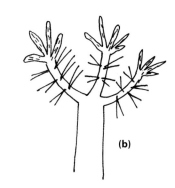

(a)

(b)

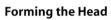
Forming a small, dense head

(c)

(d)

Forming the Head

There are two basic ways to form the head of a pine, both extensions of the techniques described previously.

For a small, dense head it is important to build up a good framework of branches early on, so the trick is to remove the leading candle of a new growth flush, and thin the lateral side candles down to three or four, pinching them back to 10 cm (4 in.) **(a)**. Continue the *midoritsumi* and *momiage* process from here, gradually building up the structure and density of the head **(b–d)**.

For a wider, more open head, allow a flush of growth to ripen over the summer, without pruning **(a)**. In the spring, cut out the leader, and thin the remaining growth to three or four side shoots. Tie these down, to well below the horizontal, to form the basis of the head **(b)** which can now be developed in the same way as side branches, pinched back **(c)** to encourage branching **(d)** and to build up density around the outside of the head. Remember that unless you can see down into the top of the tree, it does not matter if the centre of the head is 'hollow' **(e)**, as it will be concealed on all sides.

Jari Eikenaar at work on a
***Pinus sylvestris.* England.**

Even trees as large as this are pruned at least once a year. Ritsurin-koen, Takamatsu.

Forming a wider, more open head

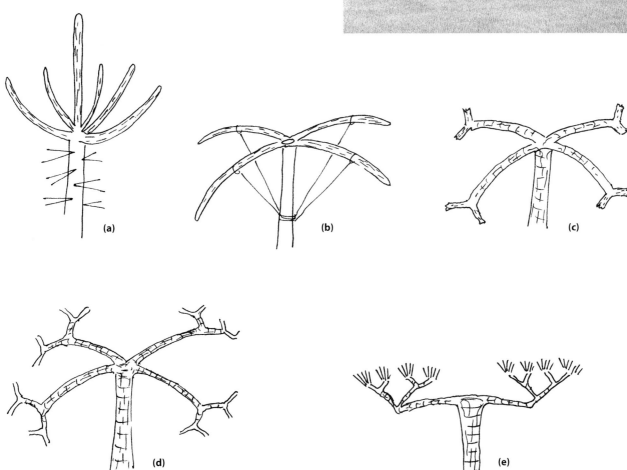

(a)

(b)

(c)

(d)

(e)

Rhododendron obtusum in full flower, surrounding *Ilex crenata*. A private hospital, Hakone.

5
Azaleas and *Karikomi*

While the pine is the most important tree in the garden, the title of Most Commonly Planted might well go to the evergreen azalea. Under various guises it appears in one form or another in virtually every garden in Japan, normally clipped into a style known as *karikomi*, the ubiquitous organic blobs that occupy the ground level of so many gardens like droplets of mercury.

The wide range of *Rhododendron* species and cultivars introduced from Japan over the years are well known. Gardens in parts of Europe and North America with suitable soil and climate have become famous for their collections, which are usually renowned for their diversity and range of flower colour, form and size. Yet typically, Japanese gardeners seem blissfully unaware of their country's contribution to the gardens of the rest of the world, concentrating instead on the traditional favourites.

The most common azaleas seen in gardens in Japan are the two evergreen forms, known as *tsutsuji* and *satsuki*. *Rhododendron obtusum* (*tsutsuji*) grows to about 3 m (10 ft.) with red flowers in May. It is the dominant parent in the hybrid varieties known as Kurume azaleas, named after the city of Kurume in Kyushu where much of the breeding work was carried out. Although the plants are evergreen, in colder parts of the country the leaves can turn a reddish colour over the winter. *R. indicum* (*satsuki*) is a smaller plant, rarely larger than 90 cm (3 ft.). It flowers after *R. obtusum*, in June, and is noticeable for its mixed colours (reds, whites and pinks) that can sometimes appear on the same plant. Interestingly, the name *satsuki* refers to it flowering in the fifth month, which in the old Japanese calendar was a month later than it is now.

In addition to these two evergreen varieties, *Rhododendron japonicum* (*rengetsutsuji*), a deciduous azalea, is also found in Japanese gardens. This is a parent of the Mollis Group of azaleas, and flowers before leaf growth begins. *Rhododendron kaempferi* (*yamatsutsuji*), another deciduous azalea, is sometimes seen as a larger specimen tree.

For the gardener who is seeking to grow azaleas in the Japanese style, wading through all of this information may become confusing. A more streamlined approach is to look for small-leaved, evergreen azaleas (ideally reaching 90–120 cm [3–4 ft.] high) with the flower colour of your choice. A trawl through *The Hillier Manual of Trees and Shrubs* (1998) produces a few worth looking out for: *Rhododendron* 'Hinomayo' with pink flowers and 'Hinode Giri' with crimson flowers both come to mind as being especially suitable.

Nothing can prepare Western visitors for how azaleas appear in Japanese gardens. They are moulded into tightly clipped, organic shapes: blobs, doughnuts, mushrooms, billowing lumps and bumps. Call them what you will; the plants themselves become insignificant. Instead, the forms they are clipped into—and the effects they create—are what matter.

Karikomi has been used in gardens since almost the beginning of garden history, but it became an art form in itself during the Momoyama and Edo eras, from the end of the sixteenth century. One man, Enshu Kobori, responsible for many gardens built at this time, took the approach in new directions, introducing the idea of *okarikomi*. The *o* prefix means 'large' and it refers to the use of groups of plants clipped into rounded shapes, suggesting mountains, clumps of trees, and, on a more abstract level, waves (known as *namikarikomi*). *Kokarikomi* (*ko* means 'small') refers to the use of one plant, clipped into low, rounded shapes. For the sake of this book the simple term *karikomi* will describe both styles.

Above: **Mushrooms, blobs, or doughnuts? Inventing the terminology is half the fun. Immaculately clipped azaleas, with *Juniperus chinensis* 'Kaizuka' behind. Adachi Art Museum. Shimane Prefecture.**

Above : **Tucked away in the interlocking hills. Shisen-do, Kyoto.**

Below: **The lower level of the garden. Shisen-do, Kyoto.**

As with every detail of the Japanese garden, the source and inspiration of *karikomi* is always the landscape, whether it is the real, physical landscapes of Japan itself, or the metaphysical landscapes of Buddhist philosophy. Even more so than other trees and pruning styles, *karikomi* is not something that should be considered in regard to individual specimens; the technique is at its most effective when it takes over the entire garden, and there are countless examples across Japan where this is the case. Three of my personal favourites are in Kyoto, the home of so many impressive gardens. Each one is dominated by *karikomi*.

Shisen-do

In the foothills to the northeast of Kyoto lies a very quiet temple, set among maples and bamboo groves. It has some of the most incredible *karikomi* in Japan, viewable from within the temple building and as you explore outside. From inside the temple, sitting on the veranda, you look out onto a small, flat area, of finely brushed gravel. Rather than being raked into patterns as is normally the case, this is merely brushed clean each morning, leaving the brush marks as a natural pattern. Bordering this area is a mass of low, wide, interlocking *Rhododendron obtusum*, out of which appears a small pagoda, giving the impression that the temple is peering out from the clouds high up in the mountains.

This very controlled view does nothing to prepare for what lies beyond. Making your way down a narrow path, flanked on both sides by tall, cliff-like mounds of azaleas, you emerge in the lower garden, looking across at a small pond, heavily

Above: Great banks of clipped azaleas, looming over the path. Shisen-do, Kyoto.

Right: The first clip of the year takes place in late spring. Shisen-do, Kyoto.

Below: Let your imagination run loose. Shisen-do, Kyoto.

planted with *Equisetum hymale* and *Miscanthus sinensis*. Beyond that is *Wisteria floribunda* trained over a pergola, and the only sound is the regular, hollow sound of the deer scarer, the bamboo *sozu*. Scattered around the pond, bordering this lower gravel area, is more *karikomi*, resembling boulders deposited by a glacier in some past ice age. Seemingly dropped at random, some 'boulders' lie flat while others appear to have landed clumsily, abandoned in the valley floor.

Looking back up the path reveals the most exhilarating view of all. Enormous banks of azaleas loom above the path. Smaller shapes interrupt large, graceful sweeping curves, creating outlines and contours which in turn form areas of dark shade, giving an incredible sense of depth to the picture and changing the scale from one of reality to that of the infinite. This may evoke banks of cumulo-nimbus clouds, or ravines and narrow gorges set in a cliff face.

The gardeners at Shisen-do have a great deal of work to do.

Although the garden is a quiet spot, it is also a popular place for visitors, and the gardeners like to keep things looking their best all year round. I visited once in May, just after the *tsutsuji* had flowered; the gardeners were clipping the *karikomi* for the first time in the year, removing barely 2.5 cm (1 in.) of growth. They make regular visits throughout the summer to ensure that the outlines of the azaleas are always crisp and tight.

On a personal note, Shisen-do is the place I associate with an extraordinary story I heard from an English teacher friend, who lived barely a minute from the temple. He told me how one summer morning he had opened his bedroom cupboard to discover a 1.5-m (5-ft.) bamboo shoot growing through the *tatami* matting. It had not been there the day before, but so vigorous was the growth of bamboo that it had pushed through the floor and shot up overnight. Apparently this is a common experience for those living in old houses on the edge of bamboo groves, but it must have come as quite a shock.

Above: **Looking out at the garden, with Mount Hiei in the distance. Shoden-ji, Kyoto.**

Right: **The uncompromising minimalism achieves an enormous sense of depth. Shoden-ji, Kyoto.**

Shoden-ji

In contrast to Shisen-do, the garden at Shoden-ji is a simple affair, situated up in the hills to the northwest of the city. Almost every garden in Kyoto could lay claim to some sort of a title, but surely this place is one of the most extraordinary. Here, a small area of raked gravel is viewed from within the temple building, framed on three sides by a low wall, capped with tiles. At the rear of the empty space, beneath the wall, lie three groups of clipped azaleas, arranged in batches of three, five and seven running from left to right. These numbers are considered to be lucky, representing a continuation of the Buddhist trilogy. (The total, fifteen, is the same number as the amount of rocks used in the famous garden at Ryoan-ji.) Nowhere else in Japan are plants used in such an uncompromisingly minimalistic, design-orientated way. In contrast to the tactile, emotional nature of gardens like Shisen-do, this garden alludes to a far more detached and abstract landscape, stirring up a sense buried deep in the subconscious.

Beyond the wall of the garden is a view of Mount Hiei across Kyoto, framed by cryptomerias and maples. This view of the distant landscape adds an important extra dimension to the garden, confounding the viewer's sense of scale. Smaller than a tennis court (actually it is 287 sq. m, or 343 sq. yd), it appears to occupy an enormous, almost infinite space. This trick of borrowing views from the landscape is known in Japanese as *shakkei*. It relies not merely on a distant view, but also on the middle ground that links the garden with that view, in this case the wooded hills on either side which slope down into a V shape, framing the mountain beyond.

The azaleas themselves are interlocking and overlapping.

This creates the outlines and shadows that not only strengthen their sculptural form, but also further enhances the sense of endless perspective. The simplicity of the wall and the regularity of the tiles only add to this effect, having no distracting details to catch your attention and thus break the spell.

Shoden-ji is renowned as a great place for moon viewing, an activity not dissimilar to cherry blossom viewing. The harvest moon in October is meant to be particularly impressive, flooding the garden with surreal light, adding further to the ambiguous sense of scale. Whenever you visit, though, it never seems to be busy, enabling you to really appreciate the tranquillity and unique spatial effects.

Konpuku-ji

Everyone has their favourite garden, remembered for various aesthetic and emotional reasons, and Konpuku-ji is mine. It is a small garden, located near many better-known, more frequently visited ones in the northeast of Kyoto, but it has one of the finest displays of *karikomi* I have come across. The first time I visited I was alone in the garden on a lovely May morning, while crowds jostled for better views at the more renowned Ginkaku-ji, barely a ten-minute walk away.

Like many Kyoto temples, Konpuku-ji is nestled in the foothills that surround the city. Reaching it involves walking through a quiet neighbourhood, rising slowly into the hills. The garden itself is behind the temple building. There is a small area of raked gravel outside the main building, which

Above: The tea house. Konpuku-ji, Kyoto.

Above right: The larger shapes of azaleas at the bottom of the slope combine with the much smaller ones beyond to stretch out the perspective. Konpuku-ji, Kyoto.

Above: As you look down on the garden, the true scale of the *Podocarpus macrophyllus* specimen is revealed.

leads to a slope that continues up into the hills. This slope is covered with azaleas, planted and clipped to evoke a scene of misty, tree-clad hillsides. Beyond that are the strong horizontal lines of three interlocking hedges, behind which lurks the straw roof of a small tea house, where the seventeenth-century *haiku* poet Basho once stayed.

The azaleas are clipped into various sizes, using the slope of the hill to evoke the sense of higher mountains in the background. The largest shapes are in the middle ground, behind which lie smaller, more compact blobs, lumps and bumps. The use of smaller forms behind larger ones creates a sense of the landscape receding into the distance.

The placing of smaller forms in the background to create an illusion of great space and depth is a particularly Japanese trick of perspective, influenced by the surrounding landscape. If the whole bank were planted with one unbroken mass of azaleas clipped into a solid carpet, the sense of scale would be far less significant than it is. It is the shadows, the dark spaces created by the outlines of the various blobs, that create this energy.

From the top of the garden, looking down towards the temple, the sense of distance is perhaps even greater than when one looks up from below. The enormous *Podocarpus macrophyllus* specimen standing among the azaleas seems to link the two levels, and the solitary rock in the raked gravel, barely noticeable from ground level, suddenly takes on significance, suggesting an island out at sea, off the tree-covered mainland.

I spoke to the priest of this temple, who told me that he took on all of the azalea clipping himself—no mean feat, as he appeared to be in his sixties. The larger trees, particularly the enormous podocarp, are handled by a team of gardeners who come in once a year for a big clean-up. This explains the relaxed atmosphere and the slightly shabby look of the azaleas, which endow Konpuku-ji with its charm.

Above and right: Two different approaches to *karikomi* **on the streets of Kyoto.**

Pruning Azaleas

Pruning azaleas is a straightforward skill, once the timing has been mastered. Young plants, going through their formative stages, are clipped back to create dense, compact shapes. Once the overall size has been established, much will depend on the gardener's attitude towards their garden, their personal preferences and attention to detail. The gardeners at the Adachi Art Museum in Shimane Prefecture clip their azaleas once in March, and then up to eight times from June until October. (Needless to say, the Adachi Art Museum is fantastically well kept, and worth a visit any time of year.)

Use hedge shears, and treat the azaleas like *Buxus* species, or any other plant that you clip. Azaleas sprout from old wood so they can be cut hard, but ideally you should clip little and often, sticking to the outline throughout the summer. After flowering, new growth will start to conceal the flowers. It is tempting to prune this back to reveal the flowers for a while longer, but this allows the shoots with the flowers on them to become too woody, resulting in bare patches later on. To avoid all this, cut below the flower once it has finished, which allows new shoots to grow out through the summer, preserving a good, dense surface.

Creating *karikomi* on the scale seen in these Kyoto gardens takes great foresight and a strong grasp of the overall design of the garden, not to mention a lot of hard work. It is quite possible, however, to create something similar on a less ambitious scale. The use of evergreen azaleas is not compulsory; in Japan *Ilex crenata* and *Buxus macrophyllus* are occasionally seen. Yet as the country is blessed—or cursed—with largely acidic soil (and with such a large collection of native *Rhododendron*

species), it is the azaleas that are dominant. In non-acidic soil, box is a perfect substitute, and indeed many gardens in Europe achieve the Western equivalent of *karikomi* using box or yew. This European topiary, often in the form of old hedges or parterres that were neglected at some stage and later restyled in a less formal way, clearly bears similarities to *karikomi*. Yet it is fundamentally different in that it tends to be featured within Western gardens as just one element among many, rather than as a landscape in itself.

Visually, the differences between Japanese and European topiary styles are quite apparent. The Japanese aesthetic, which derives inspiration from natural landscapes, tends towards organic shapes—hence the preponderance of low and wide features such as cushions, blobs and doughnuts. Contrastingly, European topiary tends to be either more formal and geometric (favouring full circles and balls over the blob) or—as seen in cloud-pruned hedges—softer, less defined, and less intentional than *karikomi*.

Creating *Karikomi*

Growing individual (that is, *ko*) *karikomi* is a slow yet simple procedure. For this example, box is used. You may be working with a rooted cutting from the garden, a young plant, or an established box ball that you intend to enlarge; begin following these instructions at whichever point is relevant to the stage of your plant. Box tends to have one quite vigorous growth flush in late spring. Try to make formative cuts before this time, to maximize the benefits of the new growth.

1 Starting with a rooted cutting, it is important to establish a good, bushy plant right from the base. Pinch out the

The beauty of *karikomi* lies in its organic nature.

leader 5 cm (2 in.) from the bottom, to encourage new growth at this point. Later in the summer, the resulting new growth can also be pinched out.

2   In the following few years, each new flush of vertical growth must be cut back by about half, ideally in June. This may seem a waste of energy, but it is important to establish a good dense base and allow the plant to develop outwards. Naturally, it will want to grow up, but we need it to grow out instead. Cut the tips of new side growth, just enough to keep the shape but without losing too much girth.

3   You may have decided to buy some ready-grown box balls from a nursery or garden centre. These are a good way to create an immediate impact and to make it easier to design large areas of planting, as they quickly give you a good idea of how your plans will turn out. At this point, rather than using secateurs to pinch out growth, it is now time to move to long-bladed *hakaribasami*, or hedge shears, for larger plants. The longer blades allow you to start shaping the plant, creating the outlines you are after, and it is only by clipping (rather than individual cuts) that a crisp finish is obtainable. Every June, after the early spurt of growth, consolidate the shape while allowing it to gradually fill out.

4   Take care to clean up after box clipping. In recent years there has been a disease known as box blight, *Cylindrocladium*, which can affect entire gardens. Removing cut leaves (and old brown ones) from around the plant reduces the chances of this fungal disease taking hold.

Once established, box needs to be clipped twice per year. In England, Derby Day in early June is the traditional time to begin, once the early flush of growth has stopped. Avoid clipping in bright sunlight if possible, as the newly revealed foliage scorches easily. Use clean, sharp shears, and try to clip to an imaginary outline, rather than merely taking off an equal amount the whole way round. This way, you will iron out irregularities rather than following any inaccuracies from previous years. Work in a circular motion, moving around the plant, concentrating on applying the same action over and over. Imagine yourself at a potter's wheel or a lathe, working automatically, oblivious to individual quirks. Do not be afraid to cut deep into older growth to reshape; box responds well to heavy pruning and any bare patches should fill in by the end of the summer.

A good *karikomi* shape is low and wide, flat at the bottom, much like a doughnut. Ideally, the sides should taper in partially before ground level, imbuing the plant with a sense of tension, as if it were a drop of water. The beauty of *karikomi* lies in its organic nature; perfect spheres and dead-straight lines are out, and smooth, comfortable contours are in. Think interlocking hills, fruit, breasts and buttocks.

Throughout the summer, feel free to clip as often as you want in order to keep the outlines crisp and sharp. It takes almost no time to go over the tops lightly with a pair of shears. By the end of the summer, growth will have stopped; now is the time for the final clip of the year. It is worth taking care at this point because the results can be extremely satisfying, especially on frosty winter mornings. Do not cut back too hard at this time of year, though, as scars will take until the following summer to heal.

Potato *karikomi* (below) gives an idea of how a design might develop, and the results can be compared to gardens like Humon-in at Tofuku-ji, Kyoto (left). Look at how a sense of distance is created using overlapping and interlocking shapes.

Planning *Karikomi*

To create whole plantings of *karikomi*, you will need to put thought into the design process. It is generally easier (and certainly cheaper) to start with smaller plants, set out first as separate shapes but destined to merge into larger ones. If at all possible try to ensure that all your plants come from the same origin; there are several different forms of even the most common kind of box, and as multiple plants will make up a single shape it is important that growth rate, leaf shape and colour are uniform.

The process is similar to planting a hedge. Prepare the ground well (box responds well to manure and other fertilizers) and leave spaces of around 30 cm (12 in.) between plants. You might envisage areas of smaller, individual shapes, tucked in among larger forms; these individual shapes could consist of just one plant, while larger ones could involve several plants together.

Think about access for weeding and clipping. Leave narrow paths or gaps, making sure that no point will become out of reach in the future. The paths add to the sense of depth by creating shadows and outlines, and you can incorporate them into the garden as real paths, winding among the box like an organic maze.

Do not be tempted to make the shapes smaller at the front and larger at the back. We have looked at how a sense of energy and depth is created by varying the design, sometimes using larger shapes closer to the front. These may be low, wide shapes, or taller, narrower ones, obscuring views from certain points. Tantalizing glimpses, and suggestions of shapes, can be just as rewarding as seeing everything at once.

Great fun can be had planning designs like this on the kitchen table. Get a collection of potatoes in different sizes and shapes, cut them in half, and arrange them as you imagine the garden might appear. Look at your creation from table level rather than from above, to give a reasonable sense of scale. Then, indulge your creativity as you experiment with different designs. I borrowed this idea from the British sculptor Richard Long, who sometimes uses potatoes as models to introduce his stone sculptures to clients; whether or not similar exercises are used in Japan, I do not know.

6
Conifers

Japan is host to an enormous array of native conifers, with pines, cedars, firs, spruce, yews and junipers all thriving in the mountain woodlands, especially in the cooler regions further north. Within the garden, very few of these conifers are excluded completely, but along with the pines a few clear favourites are used repeatedly throughout the country.

Do not confuse the Japanese use of native conifers with conifer gardens in the West; they have nothing in common apart from one or two similar names. While Japanese gardeners favour the species and a very limited number of cultivars, Westerners with a passion for variety cannot resist trying one of everything. Take *Chamaecyparis obtusa*, for example: it is very rare in Japan to come across anything other than the true form, or the cultivar 'Breviramea', but a quick check through the RHS Plantfinder Web site (2006) lists 95 different varieties currently available for the British market. Despite many of these different forms originating in Japan, in the gardens the natural selection is considered perfectly adequate, and it is the gardener—not the breeder—who is charged with providing variation.

Cryptomeria japonica **forestry, deep in the mountains. Shikoku.**

Cryptomeria japonica

Although pines are the principal trees in Japanese gardens, and azaleas might be the most numerous, nothing else has such a presence throughout the country as *Cryptomeria japonica* (*sugi*). Vast swathes of mountainside are carpeted with it, and it makes up 40 per cent of the country's forests. (About 70 per cent of the country is forested, which means that slightly more than a quarter of the entire country is covered with this species.) Most

of the original, virgin trees are long gone, replaced by row upon row of young clones. Even now many of Japan's houses are built from wood, and as they are designed to stand for 20 or 30 years at most, timber is in huge and constant demand. In places these mountainsides are fairly grim affairs, as monoculture of any sort can be, but *C. japonica* has a certain charm to it that many conifers lack; the foliage is a bright, fresh green and the texture is interesting too, with a moss-like quality. (In fact, the distinctive moss used in Japanese gardens, *Polytrichum commune*, takes its name of *sugigoke* from the *sugi*.)

Left: Young *Cryptomeria japonica* var. *radicans* grown in the traditional *daisugi* style. Kitayama, Kyoto.

Right: Different generations of *Cryptomeria japonica* var. *radicans*. The taller trees in the background have had their trunks raised. Kitayama, Kyoto.

Around temples and shrines, particularly in the mountain areas, fabulous stands of very old trees are protected from the loggers. Further south, on the island of Yakushima, there are stands of virgin forest with enormous old specimens, the largest of which is known as Jomonsugi (referring to the Jomon era [10,000–300 BC] from which the tree is rumoured to date). This monstrous tree is barely recognizable as *Cryptomeria japonica*. Along with many others, Jomonsugi is tucked away deep in the mountains of this semi-tropical island, halfway between the mainland of Kyushu and the islands of Okinawa to the south.

Given its presence in the landscape, it is not surprising that *Cryptomeria japonica* plays an important role in the garden. Despite the array of cultivars that are popular in the West, such as *C. japonica* 'Elegans' and the slow-growing *C. japonica* 'Globulosa Nana', it is invariably the species form and various clones that are used. One common form, *C. japonica* var. *radicans*, originates from the hills to the north of Kyoto, in an area called Kitayama. Here it has traditionally been grown in a style known as *daisugi*, or *kitayamasugi*, for the production of straight poles used in the *tokonoma*, an alcove in traditional homes where scrolls and *ikebana* flower arrangements are displayed.

Unusually for a conifer, *Cryptomeria japonica* has the ability to sprout new growth from old wood (*Sequoia sempervirens* and *Taxus* species are two other examples with similar attributes). Taking advantage of this, the woodsmen in Kitayama use a version of coppicing, harvesting the trunks when they are tall enough, but never killing the tree. As these trunks grow, their side branches are stripped away, leaving only a few feet of growth at the top, to prevent the trunk from forming burrs.

This results in a very fine, flawless finish that is sought after for the *tokonoma* poles.

As the traditional forestry skills have been brushed aside by modern demands, parts of Kitayama have resorted to clear felling, abandoning the coppice system, but fortunately the gardeners and nurseries of Kyoto have retained the old skills. The name *daisugi* refers to the base (*dai*) of the trunk, which remains permanent and unchanging, while the growth above is in constant flux. Within one tree there is a remarkable sustained contrast between the old base's rock-like and passive *yin* (if you like to think in those terms), and the youthful, fresh vigour of the *yang* above.

You can see *daisugi* in temples and private gardens all around Kyoto. One solitary tree often stands alone beside the temple building, expressing an essence of the mountains, a whole hillside in one tree. Here the geometry of the buildings and the curves of the roof combine well with the vertical lines of the trunks and the organic, moss-like foliage. Elsewhere, groves of *daisugi* are planted in temple grounds, allowing the visitor to walk among the trees. It is an extraordinary feeling to be surrounded by these trees, with such enormous, solid bases, yet only as tall as young saplings.

In private gardens, you often see the tops of *daisugi* peeking out from behind walls and hedges. The heads form an extension to the wall, adding a few feet of extra screening, just enough to break up the skyline and imply privacy. One private garden I passed while exploring rural Osaka had a pair of *daisugi* so vast that they appeared to fill the entire garden; their colossal lichen-covered trunks, leaning at an angle, looked more like fossilized relics than living trees.

Above: The old base contrasts with the new growth above, on a fine *daisugi* outside a private garden. Kyoto.

Below: A common sight in the back streets of Kyoto.

Centre: A single tree evokes the atmosphere of the mountains. Daitoku-ji, Kyoto.

Above right: A grove of *daisugi* at Ryoan-ji, just coming into growth in late spring. Kyoto.

Above: Lichen-covered trunks: living fossils?

Growing *Daisugi*

Some of the *daisugi* in Kyoto gardens are hundreds of years old. To achieve the balance of base and trunk that these trees have takes many decades, but it does not take long to start the process and early results are very rewarding. For a gardener starting with a young tree, the first few stages are simple. Choosing the right tree is important; the variety *Cryptomeria japonica* var. *radicans*, which has shorter, denser branches than the true form, is favoured in Japan. It is difficult to find outside of the country, so international gardeners should look for a plant with similar characteristics. When grown from seed, some *C. japonica* can be rather loose and open, which is fine for a free-growing tree but not suitable for this process.

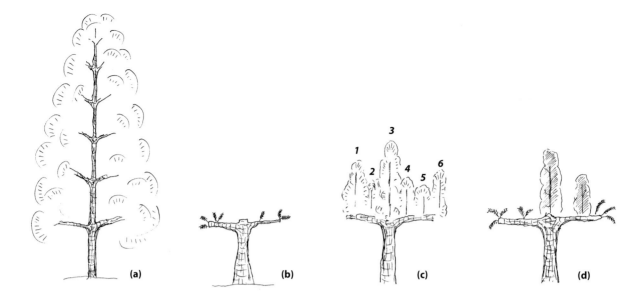

(a)　　　　(b)　　　　(c)　　　　(d)

Allow the plant to grow naturally to around 1.8 m (6 ft) **(a)**. This should only take two or three years, as it is a quick-growing tree. My friend Futoshi Yoshioka suggests waiting until the trunk is as thick as a Coca-Cola can.

1 In the spring, cut the trunk at 60 cm (2 ft.), just above a good set of side branches. Remove all the lower branches below this point, leaving just one flush, ideally growing out evenly on all sides. When cutting the trunk, pre-cut 30 cm (12 in.) or so higher than necessary, and then make the final cut lower down; this prevents the weight of the tree from splitting the trunk. Cut back the remaining side branches to 50 cm (20 in.) **(b)**, which will divert new growth further back, nearer to the trunk.

2 Over the summer the cut stump will sprout a mass of new growth **(c)**. In the autumn, or the following spring, thin out this new growth; the aim is to keep one or two shoots to become leaders, removing the rest. It helps to go about this systematically. First choose the tallest, most central shoot *3* as a new leader, and then thin out growth around it *2* and *4*. Next remove the second tallest leader *1*, which would only compete with the new leader *3* and upset the balance. Any vertical growth at the ends of the branches *6* is too far from the trunk, and should also be removed. Other growth, significantly shorter than the leader *3*, and well-spaced but not too far from the centre, will make up the secondary leader *5*. Bear in mind that your tree will have more branches than are shown in this illustration, to the front and back, and you might keep one or two more leaders at this stage.

3 Along the side branches there will be a great deal of soft, horizontal growth among the upright leaders. This is important; it will provide the new growth the following summer. Later on in the development it can be tidied up to make the branches more interesting, but for now, in the formative stages, leave as much as possible **(d)**.

4 In the autumn or following spring, repeat this process of thinning out new growth. The trick is to keep new young leaders in any empty areas *7*, and once again remove all other new growth. As the original leaders grow taller **(e)**, remove their lower side branches. This not only gives an early impression of the *daisugi* shape, but also important-ly lets in light and gives new leaders a chance to grow below. Leave the top 30 cm (12 in.) of foliage, removing everything else **(f)**.

5 In the following years, as the original leaders get taller, continue raising their trunks by removing the side branches. Leave anything from 30 to 60 cm (1–2 ft.) of foliage. Try to create a good balance between the trunks, so that the heads fit well into the overall picture. By keep-ing one or two new leaders each year, a natural order will establish itself. The top of the tree should never be flat, with more than one trunk at the same height; instead, it should be staggered **(g)**.

Eventually a time will come when the tallest trunk will become too tall for the tree. This is up to you, and the position of the tree in its surroundings, but when it seems the whole thing is becoming too top-heavy, it is time to cut out the dominant leader. This changes the dynamics

(e)

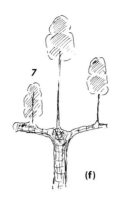

7

(f)

A *daisugi* at a nursery, not quite ready for sale. Osaka Prefecture.

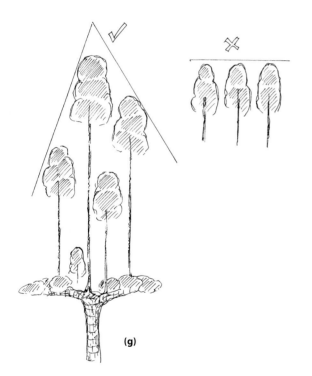

(g)

Every so often one comes across an exceptional example of a *daisugi*, one that looks more like a prehistoric relic than a living tree. These can be the original Kitayama timber trees, transplanted into gardens. The character that these trees possess is incredible, like enormous old pollarded oaks and other trees cut back regularly for firewood.

What draws me personally to *daisugi*, and to the old monsters in particular, is the balance they strike between human intervention and the natural world. The growth of the trees, like the firewood-producing pollards, is controlled by humans,

In Kitayama, *daisugi* bonsai is a local specialty.

of the tree, allowing new branches to grow in place of the old one. The original trunk at the bottom will be becoming more established, while the arrangement above will be constantly changing. In some positions, *daisugi* are grown very tall, sometimes to 9 m (30 ft.), but they can also be kept as short as 3 m (10 ft.).

Left: *Cryptomeria japonica* pruned to resemble its natural growth. Kyoto.

Below: Thinning tall *Cryptomeria japonica*, part of a screen to a private house. Kyoto.

yet within these confines they remain irrevocably natural. The same goes for all *niwaki*, but *daisugi* have a simplicity to them, a directness that I find fascinating. The British sculptor David Nash, referring to the remarkable yew *twmps* at Powis Castle in Wales, notes the distinction between naturally growing yew trees, untouched by human hands, and the clipped *twmps*, "full of human intervention…it is this sustained human presence that makes the *twmps* stepping-stones between us and the otherwise remote, and independent, world of plants" (Gooding and Furlong 2002).

The *daisugi* style is associated with Kyoto, as the trees were first grown in the Kitayama Mountains near the city. Although they are now grown further afield than their hometown, it is unusual to see them in Tokyo. *Cryptomeria japonica* is used in other styles all over the country, however, where it is pruned to represent free-growing trees. It is often sculpted into tall, spire-like shapes, the side branches cut back each year. In some gardens the foliage is sparse, cut back and thinned hard; elsewhere the texture of the foliage is encouraged by building up a deeper, more solid layer, resembling more closely the wild trees of the mountains.

Its height and speed of growth make *Cryptomeria japonica* a popular choice for use as screening, whether it is allowed to grow naturally or thinned to let light through. Whichever style or technique is applied, the trees are always tidied up every year, the old brown foliage around the trunk picked off to open up the tree. The more intensive the work on a tree, the more natural flaws like this become apparent, and although the brown foliage is part of a natural cycle, and in other situations could be overlooked, it can ruin the tree's appearance.

Podocarpus macrophyllus

Podocarpus macrophyllus is a handsome conifer, related to the yew (*Taxus* species) although the leaves are larger (and less like needles). It plays a prominent role in the garden, grown in a variety of styles, normally trained and clipped into shape but sometimes remaining as a free-growing tree. The Japanese name *maki* is generally used to describe the species (also called *inumaki*) and *P. macrophyllus* var. *maki* is called *rakanmaki*. It is the longer, darker leaf of the *inumaki* that is seen more often in the garden, where large ones can reach as much as 15 m (50 ft.) tall, although for *niwaki* 3–6 m (10–20 ft.) is more typical. It makes a fine hedge and has traditionally been used as a windbreak for *mikan* (satsuma) growers. It is also surprisingly resistant to salt-laden winds and is often grown in coastal areas.

Podocarpus macrophyllus, like its cousin the yew, sprouts very well from old wood, and is often grown in the *fukinaoshi* style. Old, free-growing trees are cut back hard, and the new growth is trained into shape. This results in trunks of considerably greater girth, in proportion to their height, than is normal. The bark of these trunks is similar to that of the yew, an attractive, peeling, slightly reddish colour.

The foliage of *Podocarpus macrophyllus* (above) is longer, and a richer green that that of *P. macrophyllus* var. *maki* (below).

Above: *Podocarpus macrophyllus* is a common sight in suburban front gardens. Osaka Prefecture.

Below: An unusually shaped *Podocarpus macrophyllus* specimen. Osaka Prefecture.

Often used in private gardens, *Podocarpus macrophyllus* has the advantage of being faster growing and easier to care for than the pine, and so is a cheaper investment for the owner. Thanks to its foliage it is a far more attractive tree than *Ilex crenata*, although in outline the two often appear similar. Training into shape is straightforward, and trees acting as screens in front gardens often have limbs trained along bamboo poles to block certain viewpoints.

Along with pines, *Podocarpus macrophyllus* is often used in the *monkaburi* style over gateways, where a branch is trained above the gate, or sometimes driveway, of the house.

A huge old specimen of *Podocarpus macrophyllus* at a nursery. Work is still being done on some of the branches. Nara Prefecture.

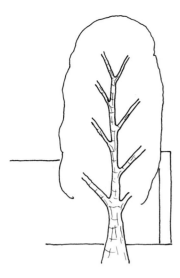
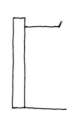

Monkaburi: before and after

Nurseries prepare ready-made trees in this style—rather bizarre-looking, lopsided things that look lost out of the context of the garden gateway.

Though traditionally *Podocarpus macrophyllus* and *Pinus* species fill this role, almost any evergreen would achieve the same effect. The process of training a branch like this is relatively simple—merely an extension of basic techniques. Branches trained in the *monkaburi* style need not only frame gateways; extended branches can be grown over lanterns, waterfalls and ponds using the same technique.

The rich green of this specimen of *Podocarpus macrophyllus* contrasts well with the roof tiles behind. Osaka Prefecture.

Monkaburi

For a tree already in place next to a gate or driveway, work out a practical height for the branch. This should be above head height, for access. The tree could be pruned and shaped already, or it could be free growing.

1 Find the branch that is closest to this desired height and growing in the right direction. It can be pulled into place if it is not quite in line with the gateway. Fix the fatter end of a stout bamboo pole (one long enough to span the gateway) to the trunk of the tree at the height of the selected branch, and hold the pole horizontally over the gateway. (You might need some help at this point.) Tie down the branch onto the pole, like a splint **(a)**. If the pressure of the branch pulls the pole up from the horizontal, it will need to be held in place with a guy rope.

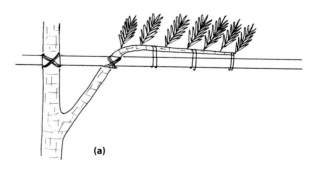

(a)

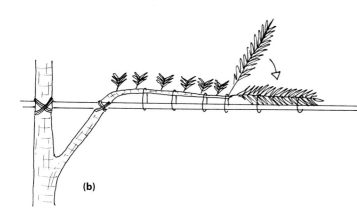

(b)

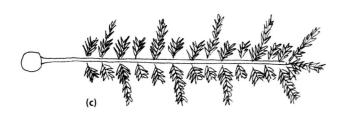

(c)

(d)

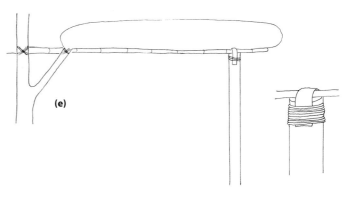

(e)

2 It is unlikely that the branch will be long enough to span the gateway immediately; it will probably take a couple of years' new growth, tied down to the pole, to reach across **(b)**.

3 Any side growth from the branch **(c)** should be cut back **(d)**, to encourage dense growth. From above, the view will eventually look like a hedge, which can be as narrow or wide as you want it to be.

4 In time, the weight of the branch may cause it to begin dropping slowly. If it becomes a problem, use a large pole as a support strut on the other side of the gateway **(e)**. Traditionally a piece of *hinoki* bark (*Chamaecyparis obtusa*) is used to lash the trunk to the pole, but a length of rubber tree tie, or even old carpet, does the same job.

Prune a shaped tree like this with shears or one-handed *hakaribasami*. Although the pruning cuts the long leaves, it does the plant no harm and is vital for achieving the crisp, clean contours that define the front gardens of private homes. In Japan pruning takes place once in mid-summer, and again in the autumn; in cooler parts of the world such as England, northern Europe and the cooler regions of North America, *Podocarpus macrophyllus* is so slow growing that one clipping, in early autumn, is all that is needed. As with all clipping, start from the top, taking as much care with the undersides of each branch as the tops, and remove any epicormic growth from around the trunk. Lower branches have a habit of catching cut clippings from above, so give the tree a good shake after finishing each branch, and at the end of the job.

These bold, sculptural caricatures of trees are not the only shapes assumed by *Podocarpus macrophyllus*; in tea gardens and *tsuboniwa* the trees often appear in a more subtle, apparently natural form. The main difference is that the trees are thinned rather than clipped, and there is less definition in the branch structure. The long, shiny leaves have a graceful habit, helping to create the softer, more natural feel that these gardens strive to achieve. Despite seeming less manmade than other styles, they are equally high-maintenance, as the thinning process

Above: *Juniperus chinensis* 'Kaizuka'. Kyoto.

Right: The natural growth of *Juniperus chinensis* 'Kaizuka' is instantly recognizable.

is a time-consuming one, and all the old leaves need pulling off by hand. The subtlety in this level of intervention is extraordinary, and—rather like pine pruning—it is an art in itself.

I have a special bond with *Podocarpus macrophyllus*. One memory comes vividly to mind: it was October 1999 in the Yoshioka nursery near Nara. We were clipping their field of *maki* for the winter, and I felt I deserved a break. I climbed to the top of my *kyatatsu* tripod ladder, peering out from the top of the tree. The sun was going down; it was a lovely, warm afternoon, and all I could hear was the snipping noises of my workmates. Looking out over the tops of so many trees was like looking out over tropical rainforest, only on a Lilliputian scale. The low sun lit up the heads of individual trees, which seemed to disappear into the mountains in the background. Up that ladder, on that day, I made the decision to spend my life learning about and growing *niwaki*. I have a lot to thank the *maki* for.

Juniperus chinensis

Juniperus chinensis often appears as a naturally growing tree in old temple grounds. It can live to a great age, and very old specimens are sometimes seen propped up with crutches. As a *niwaki*, however, one particular cultivar is favoured over the species: *J. chinensis* 'Kaizuka'. It is sometimes known as *J. chinensis* 'Pyramidalis' in Japan (according to my beloved *Woody Plants of Japan*, for example), though as its Japanese name is *kaizuka*, and *Hillier's* describes 'Pyramidalis' as having "almost entirely juvenile, prickly, glaucous leaves", it seems sensible to stick with *J. chinensis* 'Kaizuka'.

Smaller than the species, this cultivar is typically about 3–6 m (10–20 ft.) tall, although larger ones pop up here and there. Growing naturally, they have a very distinct form; the dense, rich green foliage grows up in a wispy candy floss-like way, a bit like meringue might set. They have a tall, compact habit and are often planted in rows as screens.

Like other *Juniperus* species and many conifers, 'Kaizuka' does not grow from old wood; that is, if cut back hard, it will not resprout from an area where foliage has stopped growing (typically wood that is two to three years old). This is essential information for pruning any tree, influencing the techniques and styles that can be applied. For example, *fukinaoshi*, the cutting back to a framework of branches, would almost definitely kill 'Kaizuka'. In fact, cutting back too hard even within green growth is also detrimental, provoking new, juvenile foliage that is grey and prickly.

Some Japanese gardeners are loath to use secateurs or scissors when pruning these trees, pinching out growth by hand instead. I never fully understood their reasons, but I can think of two possible explanations. Firstly, by relying solely on their hands, there is no danger of cutting back too far, into old wood. Secondly, one gardener told me that certain properties in steel are bad for the foliage and should be avoided. This notion seemed to be confirmed by other gardeners who only use stainless steel tools when pruning junipers. That said, most pruning is carried out with *karikomibasami* hedge shears—and I once worked in a garden where a hedge was pruned with a petrol-driven hedge trimmer. My interpretation is to take great care when pruning and never end up in a position where you need to prune back too hard. Think ahead and prune regularly.

Various examples of trees pruned in the *tamazukuri* style. *Juniperus chinensis* 'Kaizuka'.

With all these cautionary tales, you might think that Japanese gardeners would have phased out 'Kaizuka' through a sort of natural selection; in reality, though, it is one of the most commonly used trees. It is most often seen in private gardens, where it is usually grown in the *tamazukuri* (ball) style, and within this style there seems to be much room for interpretation. The two most basic styles of *tamazukuri* differ mainly in their density.

The denser style is just as it sounds: dense. Imagine a model of a tree, constructed out of Ping-Pong balls glued to a trunk. The result has much in common with a raspberry or a mulberry. The natural branch structure of the tree remains, but each branch is clipped into a rounded end (imagine the Ping-Pong ball). These round shapes can be more blob-like, stretched horizontally, or they can be perfectly spherical, and in some cases become much more organic and free-form. The second clearly defined shape of *tamazukuri* is effectively the same, only hollower. Here, branches are thinned, creating a more open form, with individual branches clipped into shape, with space around them. This style is often seen in rows on the boundaries of private gardens, acting as screening while allowing some light though. The scale of hollowness to density, coupled with the variously shaped branches, leaves room for an infinite number of variations—ensuring no two trees look exactly alike.

Growing *Juniperus chinensis* in these styles is straightforward enough, once you have grasped the fact that the trees resent heavy pruning. In cooler climates, however, *J. chinensis* tends to be so slow growing that you may want to use a substitute. *Cupressus macrocarpa* works very well in its place, with similar rich green foliage. However, this tree also has its drawbacks. Like 'Kaizuka', *Cupressus* species dislike being pruned

Cupressus glabra (above) and C. macrocarpa (right) are worthy alternatives to Juniperus chinensis 'Kaizuka'. England.

too heavily, so it is essential to clip little and often. Transplanted from its natural habitat of Monterey on the Californian coast, C. *macrocarpa* grows extraordinarily quickly in cooler, wetter areas, and as a result it needs pruning at least three times a year. Another alternative would be C. *glabra*. With its grey foliage this tree would be unusual in Japan, but fits in well with some Western gardens and is slightly slower-growing than C. *macrocarpa*. *Chamaecyparis* species (both the Japanese and American natives) are suitable, as are *Thuja* species. However, I would avoid ×*Cupressocyparis leylandii* at all costs.

Tamazukuri

Begin with a young plant, and treat it as though it is destined to become an obelisk-shaped topiary. Do little except for pinching out any vigorous side growth for the first few years **(a)**. As it grows, keep pinching out these sides to start building up density. Leave the leader alone—unless it forks, in which case you should cut out one fork leaving a single leader.

As you start to achieve the desired width, begin shaping the side branches with shears, treating them exactly as if you were shaping topiary or even pruning a young hedge. As you do so, work towards creating depth in the surface, cutting in around each branch to begin forming the lumps and bumps characterizing the raspberry-like form that you are after **(b)**. Depending on the speed of growth, clip two or three times through the growing season (from late spring until early autumn). As the leader approaches the desired height, it too should be clipped back to thicken the head.

From here, the next two years or so will involve consolidating the shape, clipping into the crevices between branches and

The denser version of tamazukuri

highlighting the contrast between light and shade **(c)**. Work from top to bottom, giving the tree a good shake after each branch. As it takes shape, try to develop a routine for clipping—ideally ending in the autumn when you are confident that growth has finished. Keep in mind that the final clip of the year is an important one, as conifers and evergreens can look their best in the winter, when the garden is reduced to bolder, simpler outlines.

The hollower version of the *tamazukuri* style involves leaving more space around individual branches. Begin as if you were creating the denser version, but thin out unwanted branches as the shape of the tree starts to develop, as this will give the remaining ones more definition **(a)**. Remove any foliage around the trunk, so the line of individual branches is clearer; you will probably need to do this only once, as it is unlikely that this kind of conifer will sprout new epicormic growth. Gradually start clipping and shaping the ends of the branches, keeping them as small as you want **(b)**. As the individual branches are more clearly defined than in the denser version, it can take a year or two longer to achieve satisfactory results.

Cedrus deodara **in a front garden. Osaka Prefecture.**

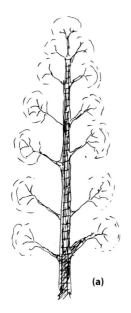

(a)

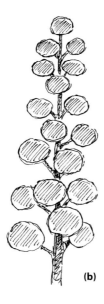

(b)

The hollower version of *tamazukuri*

Cedrus deodara

Cedrus deodara is rare among *niwaki* in that it is one of the few exotic trees used extensively in Japanese gardens. It was introduced to Japan in 1879, too late to be included in traditional temple gardens. However, it is now found throughout the country, most commonly in private gardens and municipal grounds such as schools. The graceful, slightly weeping habit of its glaucous foliage distinguishes it from native Japanese trees, but it fits into the Japanese garden comfortably. (Indeed, I suspect that it is in part due to *C. deodara*'s aesthetic contrast to Japanese native trees that it has been embraced by Japanese gardeners.) It also grows quickly and responds well to pruning—two endearing features which help to explain its popularity.

It is normally grown in one of two ways: the ever-popular *tamazukuri*, or a style known as *edasukashishitate*, which involves thinning the branches and foliage to preserve some of the natural habit of the tree. As always, *tamazukuri* can vary in the degree of density it involves, and the weeping habit of *Cedrus deodara* can become very shaggy in the build-up to

pruning, which should happen in mid-summer and then again in the autumn or early winter.

Edasukashishitate involves a combination of pruning, using elements of pollarding as well as a thinning technique known as *chirashi*. Begin by thinning branches to create a well-balanced framework **(a)**. Next, cut back the ends of the remaining branches to define the overall outline of the tree, which usually takes on a columnar shape but is sometimes broader **(b)**. New growth on these branches should be cut back twice each year. The most vigorous growth and any that is growing up or out **(c)** should be removed completely, leaving smaller, weeping shoots in place **(d)**.

Edasukashishitate

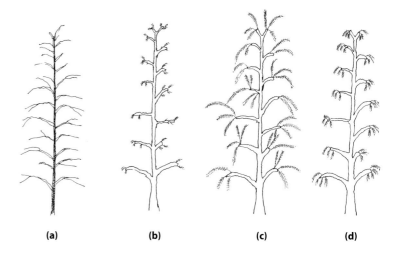

(a)   (b)   (c)   (d)

Above: Heavily thinned *Cedrus deodara*. **Osaka Prefecture.**

Below: Unusually columnar examples of *Cedrus deodara*, **with** *Juniperus chinensis* **'Kaizuka'. Shikoku.**

To encourage the tree's weeping habit, pruning is always done to a downward-facing bud or side shoot. All of the new growth that occurs further back up the branches towards the trunk is removed completely, clearing out the centre of the tree. This brings about a light, thinned effect. Over time, the ends of the branches develop swollen bolls, characteristic of old pollard trees such as *Lagerstroemia indica*. Moreover, when pruned heavily in the winter, the silhouettes of such trees can appear just like deciduous pollards—the foliage so heavily thinned, and so pale in colour, that it is barely visible.

In England and other cooler regions, where several of the conifers in this book grow so slowly, *Cedrus deodara* can be an excellent plant with which to experiment. Whereas *Podocarpus macrophyllus* or *Juniperus chinensis* 'Kaizuka' can take decades to grow into good-sized trees, *C. deodara* can yield satisfying results just five to ten years after you begin working on a young tree. Remember that it is not the fact that a tree is Japanese that makes it appear Japanese; rather, it is the fact that it has been grown as a *niwaki*, in the Japanese style. Using proven and reliable trees in your area, and applying *niwaki* principles to them, can sometimes prove more rewarding than struggling with rare and unusual trees that are exotic or interesting botanically, but for some reason are never really happy in their new home.

Taxus cuspidata

The Japanese yew *Taxus cuspidata* and the common garden variety *T. cuspidata* var. *nana* (*kyaraboku*) are seen in gardens in the colder parts of Japan, typically in the Kanto region (the Tokyo area) and further north. *Taxus cuspidata* differs very slightly from the English yew, *T. baccata*, in that its leaves are slightly more ascending, rather than flat. The two species were crossed at the beginning of the twentieth century to produce *T.* ×*media*, combining the hardiness of *T. cuspidata* with the flatter foliage of *T. baccata*.

The *nana* form is more commonly grown as a *niwaki*, sometimes reaching 3 m (10 ft.) tall, although it is usually smaller. Typically it is grown as a low, wide tree with a twisted trunk, trained at a young age when still flexible and then clipped regularly. It is also sometimes used as an alternative to evergreen azaleas, clipped into *karikomi*.

Despite being a common tree in Japanese gardens, *Taxus cuspidata* var. *nana* has no unique qualities that make it stand out as a *niwaki*. However, *Taxus* species are so well known in Europe and North America that Western gardeners—accustomed to their virtues as hedging, topiary and specimen trees—would do well to think of them when setting out on any Japanese

project. Because yew is so obliging, the pruner can choose from a variety of techniques, such as *fukinaoshi*, or the technique described above on *Juniperus chinensis* 'Kaizuka', where the form is slowly developed through a combination of modelling and carving.

When working with younger plants, you have the advantage of being able to train the trunk, introducing the characteristic bends and horizontal branches that give *niwaki* the appearance of maturity that Japanese growers strive to achieve. Use the method described in Chapter 3 to train the main trunk and tie down the side branches. It is a slow process, but—as people often realize when growing a yew hedge—once it gets going it will move along more quickly than originally thought. When the form starts developing, it is fine to cut through the individual leaves with shears, creating the smooth surface that a well-clipped tree should have. Generally *Taxus* species are slow growing enough to need clipping just once a year, normally at the end of summer. This can result in some rather woolly-looking topiary by August, and depending on individual preferences it can be worth clipping twice, once earlier in the summer and then again in early autumn.

Other Conifers

Grouping the remaining coniferous *niwaki* in a single section might appear insulting, and one or two of them might feel they have reason to complain, but the fact is that none of the following trees have quite the same presence in the garden as the few already mentioned. *Chamaecyparis obtusa* and the cultivar *C. obtusa* 'Breviramea' are perhaps the most common. The species is heavily planted as a timber tree alongside *Cryptomeria japonica*. Its water-resistant wood is used to make traditional bathtubs and sake drinking cups. In the garden it is sometimes seen clipped into large columnar and obelisk shapes. However, it is the smaller cultivar 'Breviramea' that is more common, especially further north in areas like Yamagata Prefecture. The natural habit of this tree is tall and thin, like the species. The foliage, however, is denser and grows in a horizontal, flattened way, which in some regions is thinned to optimize its appearance. In other regions a tall, thin version of *tamazukuri* is used, introducing a vertical element into the garden.

Chamaecyparis pisifera is occasionally grown like *C. obtusa*, but more often the weeping form *C. pisifera* 'Filifera' (*hiyokuhiba*) is seen, cultivated in the *edasukashishitate* style like *Cedrus deodara*. The weeping habit is maintained by pruning out upwards and outwards growth, and then thinning the remaining weeping shoots.

Chamaecyparis obtusa
'Breviramea', thinned (above)
and clipped in a *tamazukuri*
style typically found in
Yamagata Prefecture
(above right).

One of Japan's more unusual conifers is *Sciadopitys verticillata*, which is native to the mountains of Wakayama Prefecture and particularly common around Mount Koya (hence its Japanese name, *koyamaki*), where the tree is used in virtually every garden, pruned only very slightly to keep the natural shape neat and tidy. It is rarely used outside of Wakayama, which, although not far from Kyoto, is even today an isolated, mountainous area.

Ginkgo biloba appears frequently as a free-growing tree in shrines and temples, where enormous old specimens are as important as the buildings themselves. Though occasionally used as a garden tree, it is best known as a street tree. A few others worthy of a mention are *Juniperus procumbens*, *Abies firma* and *Tsuga sieboldii*, all of which make the odd appearance in gardens, but are not included frequently enough to be considered significant.

Ginkgo biloba **as a street tree**
in Kyoto. The trees are pruned
this heavily in areas prone to
typhoons.

7
Broadleaved Evergreens

From a *niwaki* point of view, nowhere are Japan's extraordinary botanical riches more evident than in its vast collection of native broadleaved evergreen trees, growing in woodland called *shoyojurin* in the warmer parts of the country. As garden trees in temple gardens, they tend to play second fiddle to the pines and podocarps, but in the private gardens—the *tsuboniwa* and front gardens all over Japan—they come into their own. Oaks and their relatives, in particular *Quercus phillyreoides*, *Q. myrsinifolia*, *Q. acuta*, *Castanopsis cuspidata* and *Lithocarpus edulis*; hollies such as *Ilex integra* and *I. crenata*; *Osmanthus fragrans* and *O. heterophyllus*; and of course *Camellia japonica*, all appear regularly in various shapes and forms.

All too often they are overlooked and ignored in Western books on Japanese gardens, where they are often dismissed as 'clipped evergreens' as though they are some lower caste unworthy of further investigation. While it might be true that they are not in the same realm as pines when it comes to specimen trees, they are an integral part of most gardens; in fact, Japanese language books on the subject always list evergreens before any deciduous trees (but after the conifers), such is their importance.

Oaks

The oaks are perhaps the most interesting of all the evergreens; there is such variety, even without including the deciduous species. The Japanese name for oaks in general is *kashi*; for linguistic reasons, the *k* sometimes changes to a *g* when it is prefixed by something, as in the case of *Quercus phillyreoides*

***Quercus phillyreoides*. Imperial palace, Kyoto.**

(*ubamegashi*), a tough, salt-resistant oak with dark, furrowed bark that is often seen as a trained, clipped specimen.

The first one I came across was at a nursery, right in the middle of the *fukinaoshi* process, which to my uninitiated eyes looked rather extreme. A trunk, perhaps 3.6 m (12 ft.) high, with a girth of 60 cm (24 in.), stood in the ground. It had undergone the first part of its treatment (the removal of virtually all side branches) some time ago, and had had time to resprout up the entire length of the trunk. At the time of my arrival most of this new growth had already been thinned out, leaving only what was needed to retrain the new shaped tree. (I recommend not removing all this growth at once, but working up the tree, only removing excess branches as each correct one is chosen. Experienced nursery workers, however, know instinctively what to discard and what to keep, and waste no time making the decision.)

Left: *Quercus phillyreoides,* in a bit of a mess following *fukinaoshi.* Osaka Prefecture.

Right: Broccoli-like *Quercus phillyreoides.* Imperial palace, Tokyo.

Our job that day was to retrain these new, flexible branches, and I was amazed at the speed and certainty with which my mentor for the day worked. (I was never allowed to work unassisted, apart from weeding and watering duties). The end result looked like a mess, but all around were other trees in various stages of the process, and the transition from tree to carcass and back to (garden) tree again became clear to me. It did, however, take me weeks to learn the identity of the particular tree on which we were working. Though everyone referred to it as *bame,* I could find no reference to this in my collection of books on the subject. Eventually, though, it finally clicked: *bame* was in fact *ubamegashi.* This sort of colloquialism is typical of Japanese gardeners and growers; they never use botanical names, and rarely even seem to stick to the full common Japanese name—and why should they? Their form of gardening is not about collecting and identifying plants, but rather about exploring the endless possibilities of working within a familiar formula.

The Mediterranean holm oak (*Quercus ilex*) is similar in appearance to *Q. phillyreoides,* and in Europe is recognized as one of the best formal topiary plants, often seen clipped into formal lollipops and large mushroom shapes. It is an ideal tree to train and prune into shape, either in the *fukinaoshi* style or starting from scratch with a young plant. It ticks all the right boxes as suitable material: evergreen, relatively small leaves, sprouts well from pruning, and not too slow growing. Unlike some of the Japanese oaks, it is easily available in Europe.

Of the remaining oaks, *Quercus acuta* (*akagashi*) and *Q. myrsinifolia* (*shirakashi*) are commonly grown as screening trees, along with their relatives *Castanopsis cuspidata* (*tsubarajii*) and *C. cuspidata* var. *sieboldii* (*shi*). Grown as individual

Above: *Quercus ilex* in front of the author's Victorian terraced house. West Sussex, England.

Above: A side view of *Quercus acuta* grown as screening. Osaka Prefecture.

A young monk sweeping fallen leaves from *Quercus acuta*. Ryogen-in, Kyoto.

trees rather than hedges (but heavily thinned in the summer and autumn) the outline of the trunk is retained, preserving the tree-like feel that solidly clipped hedges lack. Some trees are tall and narrow, planted in rows; others are given space to grow, and in time their branches—constantly thinned and cut back—develop into fascinating spiderwebs of twists and zigzags. In the *tsuboniwa* (the back garden) these trees provide shade, and they are encouraged to grow out overhead so that light breaks through in dappled beams, silhouetting the branchwork.

This thinning is a particularly Japanese approach. In fact, although it lacks the visual subtlety and attractiveness of some styles of tree pruning, it is as essential as any other; walk through any Japanese suburban back street, and for every specimen pine welcoming guests at the main gate, there is sure to be a collection of heavily thinned evergreens standing by. Western gardeners might find the heavy thinning, especially in the autumn, slightly self-defeating. Most people want to make the most of evergreens over the winter months, and there is no reason why this kind of pruning cannot wait until the spring. In Japan, however, there is no shortage of evergreens, and the heavy thinning lets in as much light as possible.

Thinning Evergreens

The process of thinning evergreens starts with the initial thinning of branches. Because the trunk and framework are so clearly visible, thought needs to be given to the spacing of side branches. Thin out any that appear too big, or too small, for the balance of the tree. Also remove any that are growing at a strange angle, or twisted or damaged in any way. Finally, avoid too many opposite branches; instead, aim for a natural sense of irregularity.

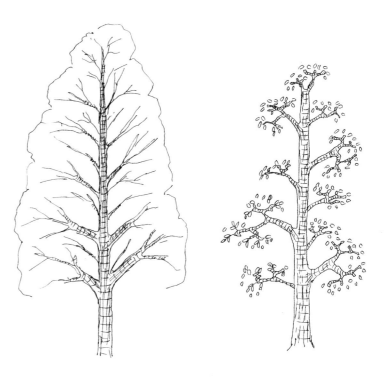

Thinning evergreens: before and after

Cut the remaining side branches back to the desired width of the tree, depending on its situation. This can be almost as narrow as a telegraph pole, or as full as the tree itself. Likewise cut the top, or allow it to grow taller, depending on the position. Thin out the resulting new growth to a fork, encouraging horizontal branching. Where there is a gap, leave new growth to fill in the space. The branches can be developed over the next few years, working towards the forking, zigzag effect. Pruning involves removing most of the new growth, leaving only a few new leaves at the end of each branch, once in summer and then again in autumn after growth has stopped.

Left: **Typical use of a tall *Ilex crenata* in this private garden. Osaka Prefecture.**

Left: ***Ilex crenata* in an unusually prominent position in Reiun-in, constructed in 1970.**

Below: ***Ilex crenata* in tree and *karikomi* form, alongside *Rhododendron indicum*, with *Cryptomeria japonica* behind.**

Hollies

The small-leaved holly *inutsuge* (*Ilex crenata*) has been in the limelight recently in the West, where it has come to epitomize the misconstrued cloud tree—an all-too-common must-have for Japanese-style gardens and trendy rooftop terraces. Yet visit the classic temple and palace gardens of Kyoto, and it is nowhere to be seen. Instead, you must explore newer temple gardens as well as private ones, to find any sign of it at all; in these more modern spaces, it appears as a multi-purpose tree, taking on various guises.

The reason behind *Ilex crenata*'s relative scarcity is simple: in Japan, there are nicer trees around that do the same job. Think of it as similar to the common privet, *Ligustrum ovalifolium*—the plant of choice for suburban hedges, but never considered in the same league as box or yew. Quite simply, *I. crenata* has none of the elegance or grace of pines, nor the rich foliage of trees such as *Juniperus chinensis* 'Kaizuka' or *Podocarpus macrophyllus*. In fact, it is rather boring. No doubt an element of snobbishness (present in all of us, after all) works against it as well.

In its favour, however, it is one of the most easily manipulated trees around, responding reliably and quickly to hard pruning and training. It is also relatively fast growing (compared to the conifers mentioned above), and tough. This makes it cheap to produce, an attractive option for many private garden owners. On top of this, it is also easier to maintain, needing only a simple clipping with shears twice in the summer.

With the arrival of imported *niwaki* in Europe, it is not surprising that *Ilex crenata* was chosen as the ambassador: cheap to produce, tough enough to survive the journey and sufficiently exotic (in the general, non-botanical sense) to create an impact. You might describe *I. crenata* as the successor to the newly introduced species brought back by the plant hunters of the nineteenth century, although this time it is the finished product that arrives, rather than the raw material. It is interesting that this importing of *niwaki* seems to be solely a European phenomenon. In North America, for example, where there is an equally keen, if not keener, interest in Japanese gardens in general, nurseries and gardeners choose to grow their own.

The European interest in imported *niwaki*, fuelled by the enormous Italian and German nurseries, came at rather a good time for Japan's nursery workers. Traditional gardening in Japan has been going through a rough patch due to the recession following the economic bubble of the 1980s, coupled with the growing popularity of the Western style of gardening, especially among women. Contemporary designers have a wider range of trees, in less defined styles, and to keep up with the changes nurseries have needed to adapt. Orders for large numbers of unwanted trees must have seemed like a blessing. (In addition to growing olives and sequoias, the Furukawa nursery where I worked had a whole field of eucalyptus, not as ornamental trees, but as fodder for koalas at a nearby zoo, so keen were they to keep ahead of the game.)

Back in the West, these imported trees end up in one of two situations: either as centrepieces for Japanese-style gardens, or as focal points in non-Japanese gardens. Ironically, they have been more successful in the latter. Used as an alternative take on traditional topiary, they work well in formal settings, flanking a door like yew cones or bay lollipops do. With the eye of the well-trained designer they can fit in as unusual focal points within the garden, framing views, lurking in borders, and generally behaving as if they have belonged there all along. It is when these imports are used in Japanese-style gardens that there is a danger that they will become the focus of attention—the only authentic *niwaki*, surrounded by unshaped plants and moving dangerously close to being a pastiche of ornaments. To avoid this, integrate them in an overall design rather than building the garden around them; aim for a design that explores a sense of the landscape, in which every tree is an intrinsic part.

Regardless of how these trees end up being used, it is how they are looked after that is most vital. There is no sight worse than a poorly clipped tree that has lost its shape and sprouted epicormic growth from every point. Even a small *inutsuge*, no taller than 90 cm (3 ft.), could be twenty (or more) years old, over which time it has been cut back, trained and clipped into shape. Following that it has been dug up, and then endured a 9600-km (6000-mile) sea voyage in a cold metal box. The least it deserves is decent care and clipping.

Above: The impressive hedge of *Camellia japonica* at Ginkaku-ji. Kyoto.

Right: *Camellia japonica* in a courtyard garden. Kyoto.

Apart from *Ilex crenata*, there are several other native hollies in Japan. The most common in the garden is *I. integra* (*mochi*), similar to the English holly (*I. aquifolium*) but with smooth leaves. It can be grown in the *tamazukuri* style (as can *I. aquifolium*), but is more interesting when grown as *daimochi*. The *dai* is the same prefix as *daisugi* (the multi-stemmed *Cryptomeria japonica*); it means 'base', and here refers to the proportions of the trunk in relation to the top of the tree. Huge old trees are grown in the hillside nurseries in the south of Japan, where they are cut down to stumps and then transplanted to working nurseries. Into these stumps are grafted strong berry-bearing cuttings of the same species, which are then trained into shape.

The result is similar in shape (though not size) to old stunted pollarded oaks, displaying an extraordinary combination of youthful growth and fat trunk below. The bark of *Ilex integra* is smooth and grey, and these cut stumps bear more than a passing resemblance to elephant legs (that are somehow miraculously sprouting leaves). A field of *daimochi* is certainly one of the more bizarre sights in Japanese nurseries; the process of grafting seems to shift the balance between man and nature in favour of man (and against the natural growth of the tree).

Camellias

Camellia japonica (*tsubaki*) and *C. sasanqua* (*sazanka*) are common plants in Japanese gardens, although not in a way that Westerners might expect. Despite the enormous array of cultivars, it is rare to ever see a collection of different types, as we are accustomed to seeing in the West. Instead, only basic variations in flower colour are used, and the plants are shaped with the *fukinaoshi* process, cut back hard and trained into shape. They also make good hedges, such as at the entrance to the Silver Pavilion, Ginkaku-ji, in Kyoto.

When it comes to pruning camellias, the skill lies in how one treats the flowers. We know enough about them in the West, but very few people actually prune them, beyond hacking them back when they start taking over the garden. *Camellia japonica* flowers in early spring, and should be pruned after that—and then again in mid-summer, after which it produces a second flush of growth. This second flush bears flowers so should not be pruned in the autumn clean-up, although quite often the flowers are sacrificed in favour of overall form. *C. sasanqua*, which flowers in the autumn, is given the same treatment. The most noticeable difference between the two lies in their flowers: *C. sasanqua* flowers drop petal by petal, while *C. japonica* flowers drop off whole, which—as every Japanese person will tell you—made them unpopular among the *samurai* class, who were put off by the similarity they saw between the flowers and their own heads.

Gardeners tend to use shears on most camellias, only using *hasami* or secateurs for the smallest plants. By cutting hard in the spring gardeners can preserve a good tight shape that would otherwise become misshapen if it were picked over by *hasami*. A great deal of care is taken when it comes to the removal of old yellow leaves, which are a particular problem in the spring when energy is being directed into fresh foliage and the older leaves are abandoned.

Left: **Great care is taken to clear up fallen evergreen leaves in late spring.**

Above: **An old specimen of *Cinnamomum camphora* outside Shoren-in, Kyoto.**

Below: **An old *Buxus sempervirens* tree is trained into shape. This one was transplanted from within the same garden. England.**

Osmanthus and Others

Often overlooked in the garden, apart from during autumn flowering, are the native *Osmanthus* species known as *mokusei*. *Osmanthus fragrans* (*ginmokusei*) and *O. fragrans* var. *aurantiacus* (*kinmokusei*) are usually clipped into large rounded, egg-shaped forms, in styles similar to that of many western shrubs. They normally flower in October, and are clipped soon afterwards, or in the following spring, with shears. As they flower on growth made over the summer, they are not pruned during mid-summer. *Osmanthus heterophyllus* (*hiiragi*) and *O. heterophyllus* 'Variegatus' are often trained and shaped like *Ilex crenata*, and look very similar to spiky-leaved hollies. Traditionally, *Osmanthus* species are planted near the toilet window, their scent masking any more earthy odours that may be escaping.

There are countless other evergreens used in the gardens: *Ternstroemia gymnanthera* (*mokkoku*), *Myrica rubra* (*yamamomo*), *Ligustrum lucidum* (*tonezumimochi*), *Daphniphyllum macropodum* (*yuzuriha*), other hollies and oaks, and more. Furthermore there are many that do not feature in the gardens themselves but are grown in temple grounds and shrines; examples include trees like *Cinnamomum camphora* (*kusu*), *Machilus thunbergii* (*tabunoki*) and *Michelia compressa* (*ogatamanoki*), as well as the smaller *Cleyera japonica* (*sakaki*). Then there are the fruit trees, such as *Eriobotrya japonica* (*biwa*), which is popular in rural areas but does not appear in temple gardens.

Outside Japan, various evergreens can be used in similar ways: *Prunus lusitanica* and *P. laurocerasus*, *Myrtus apiculata* and *M. communis*, *Viburnum tinus*, *Quercus ilex* and *Q. suber*, *Phillyrea latifolia*, *Maytenus boaria*, *Magnolia grandiflora*,

Buxus, *Ilex*, and even *Eucalyptus* species, all offer individual characteristics worth exploring. Depending on leaf size and habit, trees and shrubs can be cut back hard, then trained and clipped, or thinned in more natural styles. Many evergreen shrubs, considered to be dull yet reliable, can be treated in the same ways as small trees. As far as *niwaki* are concerned, the boundary between trees and shrubs vanishes, as the scale is determined not by natural growth but by you, the gardener.

Acer palmatum shading the
sand mounds at Honen-in,
Kyoto.

8
Deciduous Trees

Deciduous trees are an essential foil to the densely clipped shapes of the evergreens and conifers in Japanese gardens, their seasonal changes providing an element of nature that is beyond the control of the gardener's sculptural hand. While vast areas of woodland are made up of large trees such as beech (*Fagus crenata*), it is the smaller trees that are traditionally used in the gardens, and on paper the list is pretty impressive, headed by the maples and flowering cherries.

Acer palmatum

No tree has such natural grace and beauty in the Japanese garden as the maple (*Acer palmatum*). From its fresh, lime-green growth of late spring through to its fiery glow of autumn colour, it exists in some shape or form in virtually every garden across the country. The generic name is either *momiji* or *kaede*, with regional varieties such as *irohamomiji* (*A. palmatum* var. *palmatum*), *yamamomiji* (*A. palmatum* var. *matsumurae*) and *omomiji* (*A. palmatum* var. *amoenum*) named for their leaf shape, size and regional origin.

Occasionally the cut leaf dissectum form is seen, in green or purple—but generally, despite the huge wealth of varieties and cultivars available (many bred and developed in Japan) it is the true forms, as well as *Acer japonicum* and *A. shiraswanum* that are used. In the West, gardeners might fill their Japanese-style gardens with a collection of different Japanese maples, some dwarf or weeping, others dissected or variegated. Not so in Japan, where plant collecting is left to botanists rather than gardeners; in representing the landscapes of Japan, the true form is sufficient—what could be less natural than a collection of manmade cultivars? It is not until you get the chance to travel around the countryside of Japan, witnessing the natural landscapes first-hand, that this makes sense. It is always surprising to see exotic specimens of any sort, growing in their native surroundings, and maples are no exception; they thrive in mixed woodland over much of the country and are not considered the slightest bit unusual.

Temple grounds often have large groves of maples that are allowed to grow largely unchecked. They become popular tourist destinations in November as the leaves turn a brilliant red, provoking as much excitement as the spring cherry blossom. The approach to Tofuku-ji in Kyoto is a famous example, but all over the country there are hotspots (often marked on maps) that are renowned for their autumn colour. Early summer, too, is a fantastic time for maples. The new growth has opened fully, and settled down into a beautiful, fresh green

Left, top to bottom: *Acer palmatum* **in Kyoto: spring, early summer and autumn.**

Below: Lower branches float motionless like wisps of smoke. Hakusasanso, Kyoto.

colour. Walking through these groves of mature trees on the approach to temples, the effect of the silhouetted foliage overhead is mesmerizing.

Within the garden proper, and especially in the shady courtyard and tea gardens, maples are carefully manipulated to make the most of their natural shape. Branches are thinned and strong vertical growth removed, to draw attention to the spreading, floating branches. From certain views of the garden, the tree itself is hidden, with only a floating, ethereal swathe of foliage visible, suspended in among other plants. This manipulation is subtle, often unnoticeable; the aim is to enhance the natural qualities of the maple, removing any branches that ruin the elegant, horizontal branching.

An old gardener in Osaka named Kumeda-san showed me how to prune maples. He held his hand out flat with fingers apart, and explained that this was the shape to aim for when pruning the branches. He then bent his fingers into distorted positions to demonstrate how *not* to prune maples. Back then, I only ever understood a fraction of what old gardeners from around Osaka were saying to me. They conversed in a fierce local dialect known as *Kawachi-ben*, and seemed to growl as much they spoke. However, with physical demonstrations such as Kumeda-san's hand motions, as well as a good dictionary and a whole nursery full of trees to practise on, it always seemed to make sense in the end.

Kumeda-san's Maple Thinning Instructions

Start in the winter, after leaf drop and well before the sap starts rising in the spring.

1 First remove all the epicormic growth from around the trunk. This instantly tidies the tree up.

2 Next remove any strong vertical branches. These might be epicormic growth that put on a vigorous growth spurt over the summer, or shoots from the top of a side branch.

Maples have opposite buds, which means that on side

Below: **Kumeda-san's demonstration: the hand on the left shows how a well-pruned maple, with well-defined, horizontal branches, should look.**

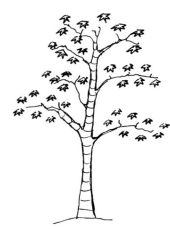

Above, left to right: **Thinning maples – before, midway through and after.**

Below: **When a branch is too upright, prune to create a more horizontal effect.**

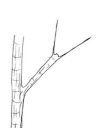

branches one set of buds tends to grow to the left and right, and the next set grow up and down. It is these up-and-down buds that can ruin things by getting in the way of branches above or below, and they should be removed.

3 These opposite buds also tend to make young, vigorous maples grow in a rather regular form, and can be thinned to give a more open look. Starting from a strong branch, remove the one directly opposite. Then work up or down the trunk, taking out alternate branches or ones that seem to crowd the overall shape.

4 If any branches are getting too long and wide-spreading, they should be cut back at a set of outward-growing buds.

5 Sometimes, however, a branch may be too upright, refusing to spread out. If this is the case, prune the branch back to a suitable set of smaller, upward/downward-growing side branches. Next remove the inward facing shoot, leaving the outward-growing one to form the new branch. This in time creates a more horizontal effect.

6 Maples rarely grow tall and straight; they usually branch quite early on. If, however, you need to encourage more branching, this can be done at any height simply by cutting the trunk. Make this cut at a bud or set of side branches, using a pruning saw if necessary.

In Japan the gardeners and nursery workers use a clever trick when transplanting maples during the summer: they pick off all the leaves, reducing transpiration and making it easier for the tree to settle in its new home. It looks miserable for a while, but if the plucking is done early enough in the summer, the tree usually puts on a second flush of foliage, which tends to have particularly vivid autumn colour, and sometimes gardeners remove the leaves of established trees purely to encourage a good autumnal show. *Bonsai* growers do similar things, on a smaller scale, although trees are usually shown seasonally, so they can afford to sacrifice summer foliage in place of stunning autumn foliage.

In other gardens, maples are shaped rather than thinned. Here the natural gracefulness is sacrificed in favour of a bolder, more sculptural look. Smaller-leaved forms give more satisfying results, as is normally the case when dense foliage is required. It is a useful style to adopt when a tree is getting too

Above: Heavily pruned *Acer palmatum* coming into growth in the spring.

Above right: Spring in Todai-ji, Nara.

Right: The Path of Philosophy, a cherry-lined canal popular for *hanami*. Kyoto.

big for its surroundings, as it is not far removed from the pollarding techniques seen on the *Lagerstroemia indica* later in this chapter. The branches are never actually trained, but with constant pruning their natural lines develop form and character. This style of maple is pruned twice in the year, once in midsummer and then again in the autumn, sacrificing some of the glory of the autumn colour.

Flowering Cherries

If I'd the knack
I'd sing like
cherry flakes falling.
—Basho, 1644–1694

To most Westerners, the flowering cherry, along with Mount Fuji and perhaps the bullet train, is a defining feature of Japan. Certainly the tree, and in particular its blossom, is considered part of the country's national identity. The fleeting beauty of its flowering season, its fragility and short life at the whim of strong winds and rain, is traditionally compared to the life of the *samurai*, who in the spirit of *bushido* must be prepared to lay down his life at any time. April in Japan ignites a frenzy of excitement and flower viewing known as *hanami*, which developed from the imperial flower viewing trips made to the hills around Yoshino, near Nara, more than one thousand years ago.

Nowadays, however, *hanami* is equally important as a social event, as for the appreciation of the blossom, and is often just a good excuse for a picnic. Many companies hold office parties in the park each spring; junior workers are sent

out in the morning to lay down blankets and reserve good spots, to be joined in the evening by workmates. Drinking and *karaoke* are the order of the day (and night), and it is seen as one of the few opportunities that working people have to really relax among colleagues. Like the autumn colour, television news updates bring the latest developments as the blossom moves up from the warmer south of the country, advising the public of the best places to see it. It is a time of great beauty, but popular spots get horrendously crowded, and it can feel more like a festival than a celebration of nature. It is this enthusiasm that defines the modern Japanese and their relationship to their landscape and nature, and it is fascinating to experience.

The species of flowering cherry most commonly seen in Japan, in the parks and along rivers, are *Prunus ×yedoensis*, *P. jamasakura* and the well-known cultivars, known in a group as *satozakura*, such as 'Tai Haku' and 'Shirofugen'. Their habit, flowering time, colour and number of petals tell them apart.

In the garden, cherry trees, in all their guises, are far less significant than would be expected, considering their impact on the country as a whole. The simple reason for this is most species dislike regular pruning, so are inappropriate for the controlled environment of many smaller gardens. Larger gardens

Left: Spring and (below left) **early summer. Todai-ji, Nara.**

Below: *Prunus pendula* 'Pendula' at Nijo-jo, Kyoto.

Right: *Prunus pendula* 'Pendula' trained over frames, in early spring and (below right) **in full flower. Kyoto.**

however, such as temple and palace grounds, are planted with flowering cherries, much as the public parks and riverbanks are. These trees are seldom pruned, and when they are it only involves the removal of dead wood. Pruning paste is normally applied to cuts to prevent infection, and most work is done in late winter, before the sap has started to rise.

The weeping cherry *Prunus pendula* 'Pendula' (*itozakura* or *shidarezakura*, the prefix *shidare* meaning 'weeping') is often seen in the larger gardens, occasionally grown over large scaffolding, to support the descending branches. They are pruned to some degree; the branches are thinned, to preserve the light flowing effect, and any non-weeping branches are removed completely. Famous examples can be found at Heian-jingu in Kyoto, best visited in early April for the full effect of the blossom. In the winter these trees are still an impressive sight, with the elaborate supporting frames and elegant tracery of the branches looking interesting, especially in the new year as the flower buds start to swell.

Left: *Prunus mume* at Kosho-ji, Kyoto. (Photo by Allan Mandell)

Above: The owner of this garden in Nara caught me peeping in to see his amazing *Prunus mume* specimen, and kindly let me in for a better look.

Prunus mume

Far more common in the gardens themselves is another species: *Prunus mume* (*ume*), the Japanese apricot, often referred to as plum. This is a smaller tree, long used in Japan but actually a native of China. It flowers earlier in the spring than most other *Prunus* species, and has always been admired for the beauty of its blossom (white, pink or red) while all around is still dormant, often half buried in snow. The fruit of this tree, *umeboshi*, is similar to an apricot, but very sour and sharp. Pickled, it is an important part of Japanese cuisine, eaten with rice as well as being used as a flavouring in *shochu*, a distilled spirit made from rice, potatoes or barley.

From the *niwaki* point of view, *Prunus mume* is a much tougher tree than many other *Prunus* species, long-lived and responding well to training and pruning. *Ume* blossom festivals take place one month earlier than cherry blossom festivals (*hanami*). More sedate affairs than *hanami*, they are held in famous spots all over the country, Yushimatenjin in Tokyo being one of the best known. The trees here have rounded heads, giving the impression of a grove of trees growing in the wild. *Prunus mume* blooms during colder weather, and the trees are often grown near the house in private gardens so that the sight and scent of blossom can be enjoyed. Typically trees are trained to lean over pathways or frame windows.

However they are used, the general aim is to exaggerate the beautiful contrast of the dark, almost black bark of older trees with the fresh blossom. The wood is hard and brittle, and any training is carried out while the plant is still young, or on fresh growth from cut wood. To direct growth in a specific direction (usually outwards), branches can be pruned back to encourage buds to break in the desired direction.

Training and Pruning *Prunus mume*

1 Start with a young tree of 1.5 m (5 ft.) **(a)**.

2 Cut out the leader to encourage an interesting shape to the trunk, then train down soft growth **(b)**, or prune to encourage good horizontal branches.

3 Cut back all the newest shoots to three or four buds. Aim for an outward-growing bud to encourage outward growth **(c, d)**.

4 The following winter, thin the resulting new growth **(e)**, and cut back again **(f)**, developing the structure of the branches.

5 Regular pruning takes place in late winter, before the blossom opens (which can be as early as February in Japan). Growth is cut back to within 15 cm (6 in.) of the old framework, sacrificing some flower buds but retaining the form of the tree and the majority of the buds **(g)** which are stronger at the base of last year's growth, nearer to the old wood. Shears can be used once branches are established, but secateurs will be needed every few years for thinning out congested branches.

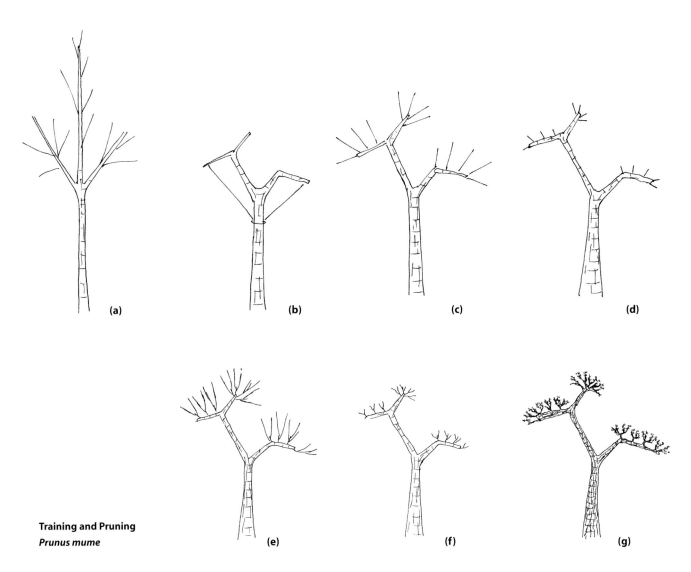

(a)　　　(b)　　　(c)　　　(d)

Training and Pruning
Prunus mume

(e)　　　(f)　　　(g)

Lagerstroemia indica

The crepe myrtle (*Lagerstroemia indica*) is a common tree in private gardens, temples and parks across Japan, where its name, *sarusuberi*, literally means 'monkey slips', in reference to its smooth, shiny bark. It is a vigorous tree, and it likes the sun. It flowers in mid-summer, usually red but occasionally white or pink.

In the garden *Lagerstroemia indica* is most often seen in pollarded form, which not only keeps the vigorous summer growth in check, but also shows off the smooth bark well, creating a strong, sculptural form of trunk and branches that looks particularly good in the warm winter light. For gardeners who only know pollarding as the practical technique of street tree pruning, the Japanese version can be a revelation. The

A young *Lagerstroemia indica* specimen in flower. Osaka Prefecture.

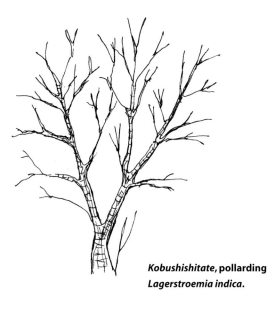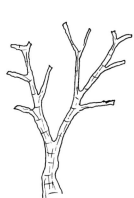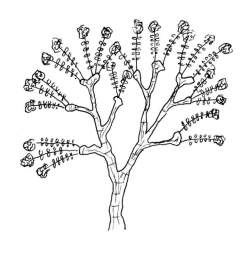

Kobushishitate, pollarding
Lagerstroemia indica.

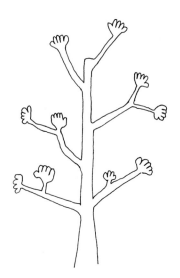

Left: *Kobushishitate* translates literally as 'fist pruning'.

Right: *Kobushishitate* pollarded *Lagerstroemia indica,* private gardens. Osaka Prefecture.

overall shape of the tree, along with its density and weight, is considered. Branches are thinned to accentuate the sculptural look, and each autumn all the current season's growth is cut off, which in time creates the characteristic bolls, or swollen branches of a pollard. The pruned bolls resemble clenched fists, giving rise to the Japanese name for this style of pollarding: *kobushishitate,* which translates literally as 'fist pruning'. The autumn colour of the *sarusuberi* is an attractive collection of yellows, oranges and reds, but often this is sacrificed in the annual prune, depending on when the gardeners are available.

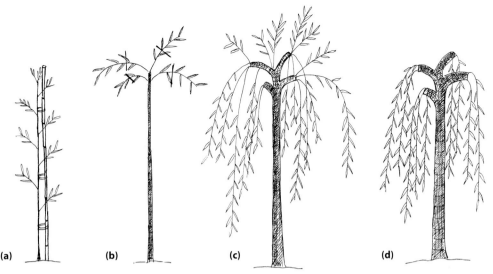

(a)   (b)   (c)   (d)

Salix babylonica: **hard pruning and heavy thinning.**

Salix babylonica

The natural habitat of the weeping willow, *Salix babylonica*, is near water, and it is usually planted alongside rivers and ponds, where it is heavily pruned to accentuate its weeping habit. Lining canals, these trees are sometimes grown with straight, clear trunks measuring 1.8–3 m (6–10 ft.), on top of which a structure of branches grows. From these branches springs the new, weeping growth that cascades down like a veil around the trunk.

To ensure a straight trunk, train the leader of young trees up a cane **(a)**. Strip the lower branches, pinch out the leader at the desired height, and cut back the top side branches to create the framework of the head **(b)**. Formative pruning is done over the winter, cutting to shape and removing unwanted branches. Once this basic pruning has been carried out, however, little work is needed apart from rigorous thinning, towards the end of summer **(c)**. From each branch only one or two weeping strands are kept on the tree—those with the tidiest habit, normally new that summer, falling gracefully from the tree **(d)**; the remainder are removed.

Willows of all sorts tend to come into growth relatively early in the year, and when these selected strands come into bud, and then into leaf, with the fresh willow-green of spring, the effect is remarkable. Over the summer, growth is vigorous, and not always weeping (some growth inevitably grows up or out). It is this growth, and the oldest of the weeping strands, that are pruned out towards the end of summer. In Japan gardeners normally try to do this in August, as September brings the threat of typhoons, which make such a mess of the delicate foliage.

Salix babylonica **in late spring. Myoren-ji, Kyoto.**

*Fujidana Wisteria floribunda,
one month apart in spring.
Kasuga Taisha, Nara.*

Other Deciduous Trees

A handful of other deciduous trees are used regularly in the Japanese garden, although none of them have a defining style, or carry as much importance in the traditional gardens. Recently, however, there has been a move towards more relaxed, informal planting in private gardens, and many of these trees, especially those with attractive flowers, are being used more frequently. For instance, *Cornus kousa* (*yamaboshi*) and its exotic cousin *C. florida* (*hanamizuki*), *Styrax japonica* (*egonoki*), and various *Magnolia* species such as *M. liliflora* (*mokuren*), *M. denudata* (*hakumokuren*) and *M. kobus* (*kobushi*) appear in these more modern gardens, and occasionally in more traditional ones. Despite all of these options, *Acer palmatum* remains the favourite in traditional and contemporary gardens, when the dappled shade of deciduous woodland is desired.

Paulownia tomentosa (*kiri*) is almost never seen in the garden, despite being commonly found in the countryside. This may be because it has large leaves and is especially fast growing, making it a difficult tree to accommodate. Or perhaps its scarcity in gardens is related to the traditional use of its timber: when a girl was born in the family, a tree would be planted, and it was thought that by the time she was married it would

be large enough to harvest to construct a wooden wardrobe for her dowry. *Kiri*, therefore, were destined for a short life.

Other larger deciduous trees such as *Celtis sinensis* (*enoki*), *Zelkova serrata* (*keyaki*) and *Cercidiphyllum japonicum* (*katsura*) are also largely absent from gardens, but are often seen growing in their natural state in parks. *Zelkova serrata* is an important street tree, its vase-like shape making it an ideal, relatively low-maintenance choice for busy city streets.

Although not trees as such, *Wisteria floribunda* (*fuji*), native to Japan, and *W. sinensis* are often grown in gardens, where they are trained over pergolas, known as *fujidana*. Over the winter months they make rather curious objects, the heavily pruned branches supported by an elaborate framework. In May, after eleven months, the wait is finally over and the long racemes open, hanging down through the pergola. The flowers of *W. floribunda* open from the top to the bottom, while those of *W. sinensis* open all at once, but the racemes tend not to be so long. Pruning wisterias trained like this is no different from pruning wisterias growing against a wall; the vigorous summer growth is cut back to 30–60 cm (1–2 ft.), and then over the winter cut back again down to two or three buds from the old framework.

9
Bamboo and Other Plants

Bamboo

Dozens of bamboo species grow in Japan. They range in size from the low *Pleioblastus* species to the huge *Phyllostachys edulis* (*mosochiku*) and *P. bambusoides* (*madake*) that can be seen in groves called *takeyabu* all over the country, reaching as tall as 18 m (60 ft.). Of all the bamboo species, it is these two giants that are most often used as raw material for horticultural and agricultural purposes.

My very first day at work with the Furukawa nursery involved going into a grove of *Phyllostachys edulis* and cutting down fifty or so canes (although the word 'cane' hardly does them justice at that size) to make into supports for a some imported olive trees. My job was to prepare 6-m (20-ft.) lengths as they were dragged into a clearing, and each cane produced two of these lengths, with the top being too spindly to use. This almost agricultural use of bamboo, rather like coppiced woodland in Europe, ensures the lasting survival of the *takeyabu*, as they continue to serve a purpose. Of course, bamboo shoots are also eaten, and *P. edulis* is considered the biggest delicacy, the new shoots being dug up before they have sprouted from the ground.

Of all the Japanese plants to have fascinated Westerners, perhaps none are more misunderstood than the bamboos. In the West bamboo is seen as a symbol of Japanese gardens, even a symbol of Japan itself, as definitive as the flowering cherry. Gardeners embarking on a Japanese-style garden include bamboo as a matter of course—and why not? It is from Japan, it is an interesting, attractive plant that never fails to make an impact, and it is easy to grow: perfect. In Japan, though, it is a different story.

Phyllostachys edulis, **with new shoots, late spring. Kyoto.**

Left: Bamboo adds a strong vertical element in the garden. Zuigan-ji, Tokushima.

Above: *Phyllostachys bambusoides* being sold as individual canes at a nursery. Osaka Prefecture.

While bamboo is a common sight in the landscape, and according to my doctrine of *niwaki* should therefore qualify as suitable garden material, it does not feature in gardens nearly as much as you might imagine. This is mostly because of its extraordinary growth habits—it is far too vigorous for the confined, carefully controlled landscapes of the garden. That is not to say that it is ignored completely; it is present in many gardens, only not to the extent Westerners might imagine.

Groves of *Phyllostachys edulis* or *P. bambusoides* sometimes grow in the grounds of temples, usually in a natural state (but no doubt farmed for food and materials). Groves that are visible from the garden proper are often pruned in some way: the tops can be cut to height, or the lower branches removed to open up or frame a view. Within the garden itself, smaller species of *Phyllostachys*, such as *P. nigra* (*kurochiku*) and *P. aurea* (*hoteichiku*) as well as *Semiarundinaria fastuosum* (*narihiradake*), are sometimes used in a very tightly controlled, clipped style. It is in the *tsuboniwa* and tea gardens that they are most prominent, where the simple atmosphere of the countryside is re-created through the use of damp, dappled woodland. Then there are the dwarf bamboos such as *Shibataea kumasaca* (*okamezasa*) and some of the *Pleioblastus* species grown as groundcover, and mown or clipped into shape, rather like icing on a cake. They can be so low as to look like lawns, while other times they resemble low masses of clipped azaleas.

To understand the pruning of bamboo it is important to grasp its growth habits. Bamboo is a grass; it grows differently from trees and woody shrubs. Spend a summer watching a clump of bamboo and several things become clear.

First of all, obviously, it is evergreen. In early summer new culms (the term for canes when they are still living) start to appear from the ground. They shoot up, quickly, for about a month. When they reach their full height (which, on all but the most mature plants, is typically slightly taller than the height of the old growth), branches open and leaves shoot from these branches. You will notice that none of the old growth actually gets any taller—culms do all their growing in one short burst—but the plants have a new flush of leaves on old branches. You will also notice, especially if the plant is in your own garden, how much mess they make during the summer. New culms come wrapped in protective sheaths—smooth, dry, papery things that are soon discarded. Then there are the old leaves on older canes, which are discarded with the arrival of the new flush of foliage. One or two canes in the clump might fail to grow new leaves; they are dead, having lived for up to eight years. Untended groves and clumps of mature bamboo often have dozens of dead canes, dry and brittle yet still standing.

How does all this affect pruning? The good news is that once an individual cane has been topped (cut at a certain point), it will never need topping again, as canes do not continue growing in following years. The bad news, however, is that

An unusual sight in a private garden. Uchiko, Shikoku.

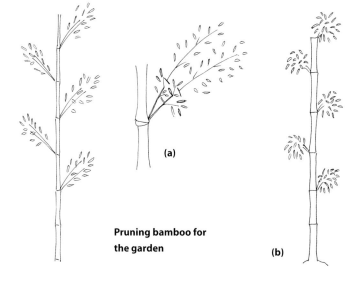

Pruning bamboo for the garden

(a)

(b)

the very next year there will be new canes, which will also need topping. The most important fact of all to remember, though, is that however unusual bamboo might seem, it is after all only a grass—and you know what to do to your lawn, don't you?

Bamboo Pruning

The simplest part of bamboo pruning is the removal of old dead canes, and any new ones that are growing out of place. They should be cut right at ground level; fresh canes will be soft, old ones surprisingly hard. This is best done in the summer, after the flush of growth, and then it should not need doing again for a year.

A more advanced process is the raising of the stems by cutting off the lower branches. Again, this is best done in the summer, when the new canes have fully opened. Raising an entire clump of bamboo does several things: it shows off the canes (some species, like *Phyllostachys aurea*, have interesting nobbly bits at the bottom), allows light to reach the ground below, and creates a strong, sculptural impact.

One step further, the tops can be cut out immediately above a flush of branches. Usually this is done to restrict the total height, but it has the side effect of forcing more energy into the side branches in future years, making them bushier and denser.

The final and most creative part of pruning is carried out when the bamboo is actually in the garden rather than merely visible from it. It involves cutting back the top as well as the side branches, so that over its lifetime a cane builds up dense clumps of leaves at each node, which are clipped like topiary.

Some bamboo responds better to this process than others. *Semiarundinaria fastuosum* is particularly suitable because it has three branches at each node, rather than the normal two, meaning that it gets bushier more quickly. On close inspection, the side branches of bamboo are simple, with clearly defined buds similar to those of woody shrubs. By cutting back to the lowest of these buds **(a)** the branch is forced to regenerate, and constant cutting back, two or three times over the summer, quickly builds up their density **(b)**.

Phyllostachys nigra. Kyoto.

Above: It may not be *niwaki* exactly, but *Chrysanthemum grandiflorum* is trained and shaped with similar attention to detail. Osaka Prefecture.

Below: A wide range of mosses thrive in the dappled shade of Saiho-ji, also known as Kokedera, the Moss Temple. Kyoto.

Not *Niwaki*

By now readers should have realized that the term *niwaki* refers to more than just trees. Shrubs and bamboos also qualify, when transformed in the garden through pruning and training. There is a limit, though; dozens of plants you might be hoping to read about do not qualify. For instance, there has been no mention of the traditional low-level garden plants such as ferns, grasses like *Acorus gramineus*, Dutch rush (*Equisetum hymale*), dragon's beard (*Ophiopogon japonicus*) or even the native Japanese grass (*Zoysia japonica*). Popular flowering plants such as hydrangea (*Hydrangea macrophylla*), irises (*Iris ensata* and others) and the tree peony (*Paeonia suffruticosa*) receive no particular attention that could define them as *niwaki*, but the amazing autumn-flowering *Chrysanthemum grandiflorum*, trained into bizarre shapes and displayed in special chrysanthemum shows all over the country, does deserve a mention, for the sculptural process it goes through. The excellent *Garden Plants of Japan* (Levy-Yamamori and Taaffe 2004) goes into more detail on all these, and many other plants.

Ironically it is moss, the very smallest of all plants used in the garden, that deserves a final credit. Certain parts of Japan—and Kyoto is a particularly famous example—have very high water tables, where mosses of all sorts thrive. One noteworthy example is found at Saiho-ji, more commonly known as Koke-dera (the Moss Temple). Originally founded in 1339, the temple and its garden have been through countless changes, having been ravaged by war, fire and flood. During the Edo era (1600–1867) when power shifted from Kyoto to Tokyo, the garden was totally neglected and the moss took over. It is now is one of the most beautiful and famous gardens in Japan, but it is also one of the most unusual, with most of its area taken up by mossy banks surrounding a pond, beneath a very natural, unpruned canopy of trees. Various species of moss grow here, and great attention is paid to their upkeep, with regular sweeping of fallen leaves. Visiting Saiho-ji is especially difficult; you have to book in advance, or go with a tour group, which involves a bit of forward planning. The effort is worthwhile though, for despite the lack of *niwaki*, the garden really is unique.

Far more typical of moss in Japanese gardens is the omnipresent *Polytrichum commune* (*sugigoke*). It takes its Japanese name from *sugi* (*Cryptomeria japonica*) and *koke* (moss, the *ko* changing to *go*) and it is easy to see why: the individual stems in a bed of moss appear like cryptomeria trees covering a mountainside. In most gardens, it tends to dry out and look pretty unhappy over the winter, but the rainy season in early summer revitalizes it, and it springs back to its luminous life. Birds can be a problem as they peck at the moss for grubs; occasionally you come across webs of fishing line suspended at waist level to discourage them.

Sugigoke is sold at nurseries in squares, rather like lawn turf. It is grown in a red clay soil called *akadama*, which protects the moss from drying out when newly planted. Perhaps inevitably, though, recently planted moss tends to look in very bad shape—it takes constant watering and the diligent removal of fallen leaves over a year or so to become established. In some gardens, the old brown needles of pine trees are collected in the autumn during the *momiage* pruning, and layered over the moss to act as a frost-proof covering for the winter.

Moss is at its most interesting when it covers the undulating lumps and bumps of landscaped gardens, mimicking the landscapes of Japan. Suddenly the name *sugigoke* takes on even more meaning, when compared with the cryptomeria-clad hills in the landscape: gardens like Shoren-in in Kyoto, with a series of soft, rounded hillocks rising up beyond the pond, surrounded by clipped azalea *karikomi* and maples, take inspiration directly from these landscapes. The twentieth-century designer Mirei Shigemori adds a postmodern twist to these moss-clad hills; for instance, in the gardens at Tofuku-ji he re-creates natural forms within the abstract framework of raked gravel and courtyard walls.

A typical use of *Polytrichum commune* among the mossy hillocks at Shoren-in. Kyoto.

The modernism of Tofuku-ji is still intrinsically linked to the landscapes of Japan.

Outside Japan, where it is difficult to buy moss, it can be substituted by *Soleirolia soleirolii* (mind-your-own-business), which creates a vivid, emerald-green effect. It turns brown over winter in colder areas, and it spreads like mad, but is the most similar groundcover to moss. In shady areas it develops a magical quality, enveloping the ground below, hiding its form like a blanket of snow. In dryer, sunny areas it is less invasive and more compact, hugging tightly to the ground as if it were hillside, grazed by sheep.

10
Behind the Scenes at Japan's Nurseries

Never overlook the role of Japan's nursery workers and gardeners. Without the nurseries there would be no *niwaki*, and without the gardeners the *niwaki* would quickly revert back to their free-growing habits and the whole point of the Japanese garden would be lost. Of course, all gardens across the world depend to some extent on the human input of gardeners and growers, but so intense is the level of human intervention in Japanese gardens, especially regarding the growing and pruning of trees, that the role of the gardeners and nursery workers is even more essential here than in other gardening cultures.

Both professions developed from labourers, known as *kawaramono*, who in the earliest days of garden making undertook the physical work of moving earth, rock and trees. These *kawaramono* took their name from the riverbanks, where they lived as a low caste in society; they were tanners, dyers, itinerants and even actors. Yet as their skills evolved, individuals came to specialize in garden construction, and became known as *sensui kawaramono*. Nowadays the gardeners (*niwashi*) and nurserymen (*uekiya*) occupy respected roles, and although these are two clearly defined jobs, they are so closely related that at times the boundaries can seem blurred.

Uekiya, the Nursery Workers

Very few trees are trained from scratch directly in the garden—the results take too long to fit satisfactorily in the landscape. Instead, the job is given to the nursery workers, the *uekiya*. (The term translates simply as 'growing tree person', the ending *ya* describing a craftsman or seller in general.) The nurseries are the starting point for the majority of *niwaki* in Japanese

Kumeda-san.

Right: A small nursery in Shikoku.

Centre right: A field of *Pinus parviflora*, surrounded by rice fields, taro plants and scarecrows. To the left are the Furukawa *Sequoia sempervirens*. Osaka Prefecture.

Below right: Enormous *Pinus parviflora* at a nursery. Osaka Prefecture.

gardens, and they come in all shapes and sizes, dealing from wholesale through to trade and down to retail customers.

My own experience involved working for a fairly large local nursery, Furukawa Teijuen, selling to landscapers, developers and councils. It was run by the Furukawa family in a very hands-on way; staff included the father and his three sons, assisted by a handful of extras (one of whom was Kumeda-san, who shared his maple pruning opinions with me). A cousin ran a spin-off garden centre, and dealt with import and export, for as well as growing a range of traditional *niwaki* the nursery also bought trees from Holland (*Picea pungens*) and Italy (*Olea europa*), sending back in return large numbers of *Ilex crenata*. Previous generations of the family had introduced *Sequoia sempervirens*, the tallest of which now tower over the surrounding nursery, adding a bizarre, Californian feel to the neighbourhood.

Routine work at the nursery, varying through the seasons, involved the planting, training, pruning and rootballing of trees. Some were bought in as established specimens ready for sale, while others were grown from seed and cuttings. They were trained as young plants, shaped and clipped over many years until deemed ready. At the nursery, most of the techniques I describe could be witnessed over the course of the year, but the one I found most fascinating was the rootballing. Virtually all plants grown in traditional nurseries are field-produced, and the methods for moving them safely are as important as any training or pruning techniques.

Nemawashi, Rootballing

There are two basic reasons for digging up a tree at a nursery: one is to sell it, and the other to prepare it for future sale. At

Left: Rootballing: in a waist-high trench, the *uekiya* is cutting roots thicker than his wrist. Most of the hard work has already been done with the help of an excavator.

Centre left: Larger trees, such as this *Podocarpus macrophyllus* specimen, are moved by crane.

Below left: *Quercus phillyreoides* waiting for collection. Osaka Prefecture.

work, we might be pruning in a pine *hatake* (the general term for nursery land, meaning field, also used for fruit and vegetable growing) when the boss would report (via mobile phone) that a customer had ordered some trees for collection that afternoon. Provided the trees were small enough to move by hand, we would set off in our mini four-wheel drive trucks (nursery workers, gardeners, carpenters, workmen—everyone drives these very practical and very small trucks at work). Upon reaching the trees we would dig them up by hand, and drive them back to the nursery. Here they would be thoroughly soaked, the rootballs covered with sacking, to await collection. Larger trees were dug with the aid of mechanical excavators, and lifted with cranes. In the old days, block and tackle with a tripod would have been used.

These trees being sold would have been transplanted regularly at the nursery, to prevent the roots from becoming too established. For gardeners accustomed to pot-grown trees, rootballing can appear savage—but cutting the roots actually causes smaller, more fibrous ones to develop, which re-establish more quickly in their new homes. Trees for sale at the nursery are not fully planted, but heeled in at ground level, with earth mounded around the rootballs like enormous molehills. Rows of trees are planted in furrows, earthed up like potatoes. (This portability has a downside, evident during the autumn typhoon season, when whole fields of newly heeled-in trees can be blown over in minutes). As trees are sold, areas of nursery are constantly rearranged to make room for new stock, and during this rearrangement leftover trees automatically become transplanted as they are reshuffled.

The sale of trees continues through the year, halted only by frozen ground. Once the trees have been rootballed for the first

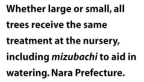

Whether large or small, all trees receive the same treatment at the nursery, including *mizubachi* to aid in watering. Nara Prefecture.

time, they can survive future movement, even in mid-summer, provided they are watered enough. Their first rootballing, however, takes place from autumn through to spring. Evergreens respond better if moved in the autumn, as they make some root growth over the winter, while deciduous trees are moved any time after their leaves drop.

To balance the loss of root, the trees are usually thinned to some degree in order to reduce foliage and transpiration. Large, deciduous trees can have as much as one-third of their smaller branches removed. Once replanted (and often trees are lifted out of the ground and replanted in the same spot there and then), the earth is raised up around the rootball in a style known as *mizubachi* (water bowl), and then watered thoroughly, the reservoir of the *mizubachi* preventing the water from running away. Many of these *hatake* are on hillsides, far from piped water, so drainage ditches are temporarily dammed, and the water pumped from the mini-reservoirs for the job. As the newcomer to the team, one of my jobs was to ensure the water supply from the drains to the trees was not blocked, un-kinking heavy-duty hose pipes, and generally getting very wet, while every one else looked on in amusement, enjoying a break.

Moving trees is one of the most valuable skills that *niwaki* enthusiasts in the West can possess. The scarcity of nurseries selling finished trees, and the time it take to grow them, means that transplanting semi-mature trees, which have already developed some of the character of older age, is the most rewarding way to make a start. In the garden, for example, there may be the remnants of an old hedge, or a piece of topiary that has long been ignored, or perhaps a windbreak of pines planted ten years ago, which now needs thinning. Having the confidence,

and the strength, to salvage these—to transform them into something new—is most rewarding. You also have the advantage of being able to plant trees at interesting angles and bend the trunks, which is so important for the character of the tree.

Conventionally, when moving trees in the West, we are told that we ought to pre-cut the rootball a year in advance to reduce the stress—the aim being to encourage the formation of new roots which will tolerate the eventual move more happily. This is true, but unless the tree is very large, or very old, this advance cutting is by no means essential. It will speed up the recovery of the tree in its new position, but of course it also slows down the actual move by a year. If the whole operation is done in one go, the tree might not recover its appearance as quickly—it probably will not put on very much new growth the following summer, for example—but it will be busy underground making new roots, establishing itself for the future.

It is important to know a bit about roots in general before getting started. Some trees, such as oaks, are deep-rooted, while others, like pines, have shallow, wide-spreading ones. This can be due to their native habitat; for instance, trees found growing in dry, stony areas in the Mediterranean tend to have deep root systems, developed for searching out water supplies. Some plants have very fibrous roots (for instance,

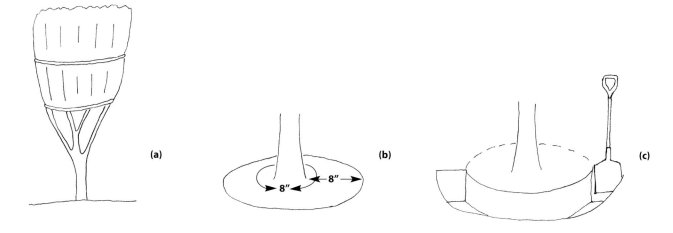

(a)

(b)

(c)

Rhododendron species and *Buxus* species), and tolerate disturbance well, but others have fewer, larger roots (pines again), and take longer to recover. The soil type is also important. Trees growing in shallow soil over a bed of heavy clay will tend to have quite shallow roots, and trees growing in very stony ground will just be hard to dig up. Some trees are notoriously reluctant transplanters—*Eucalyptus* species, for example. The long roots of *Wisteria* species, when rootballed in Japan, are never cut, but carefully dug out and wrapped around the rootball itself, such is their dislike of being moved.

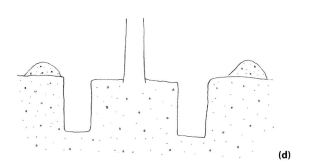

(d)

Rootballing

To move a young tree, perhaps a ten- to fifteen-year-old pine, wait until the autumn. You will need: a strong spade, an old pair of secateurs and a saw, heavy natural fibre string or rope, a strip of hessian, and a tarpaulin or several old compost bags. The process is simple, but slow, and hard work.

1 Start by tying up any low branches that will get in your way. Cut them off completely if they are not needed, and then skim off any grass and weeds around the tree **(a)**.

2 With a length of string, measure the girth of the trunk at ground level. The measurement—call it 20 cm (8 in.)—is the basis for the radius of the rootball. Use the 20-cm (8-in.) length of string to mark a circle the whole way around the base of the trunk, scratching the ground with a stick **(b)**. This is an average measurement, and can be increased or decreased, but do remember that the tree has to be lifted, and an increase of just a few inches will increase the volume and weight of the rootball considerably.

3 With your spade, cut around this circumference, as though you are edging the lawn: cut half a spit's depth, straight down, with the spade aiming outwards, away from the trunk. Now dig a trench, outside the circumference, the whole way around, as wide and deep as the head of the spade **(c)**. Cut out small chunks of earth with each cut, moving backwards, working around the circumference. Never cut into the circumference circle, but work around it. Pile up the soil on the tarpaulin or compost bags. Most of the roots you encounter can be cut with the spade, but larger ones will need a saw or secateurs (it is worth using an old pair, as inevitably they get quite rough treatment).

4 Having completed one lap, repeat, this time going wider as well as deeper, but always outwards, away from the trunk. You will need a trench about 50 cm (20 in.) wide. Continue to cut any roots that you come across **(d)**.

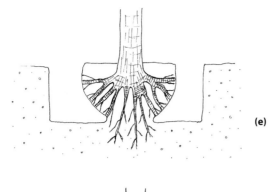

(e)

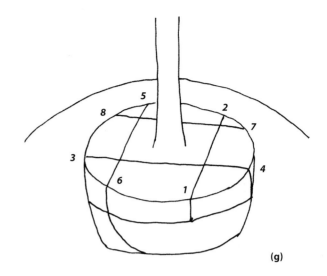

(g)

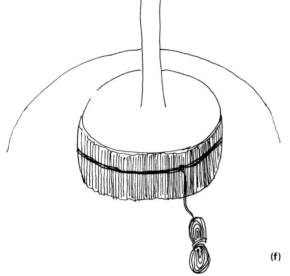

(f)

5 As your trench's depth reaches about 45 cm (18 in.), you should have a drum-shaped rootball sitting in the trench. Now gradually start undercutting. This involves digging deeper still, but gradually scraping away to make a bowl shape **(e)**. Always avoid cutting into the rootball. Use the spade like a sculptor would use a chisel, skimming small planes of earth from the rootball, slowly whittling down to a uniform shape.

6 When the rootball is balancing on a core of earth directly underneath (almost completely undercut), then it is time to wrap it using a technique known as *nemaki*. Cut any loose root ends back to the surface, and then wrap a length of hessian around the edge of the rootball, tucking it under as much as possible. Hold it in place with a length of string, but do not cut the string; instead, leave it joined to its ball **(f)**.

7 Use the same string to bind the rootball **(g)**. This is a complicated procedure that involves trying to compress the rootball, to hold it together around the roots. Keep the string in a ball, feeding it out as needed to avoid tangling. Follow the diagram **(h)**, starting at point **1** and finishing at point **8**, pulling tightly at every point to contain the rootball. The action involves crossing over the rootball (the solid line in the diagram) and then underneath (the broken line), coming up approximately 130 degrees further around, and then over, until a complete revolution has been made.

Pinus sylvestris in England, ready to be wrapped. Carving out the rootball from the earth is a very sculptural process; the more care put into it, the better the eventual outcome.

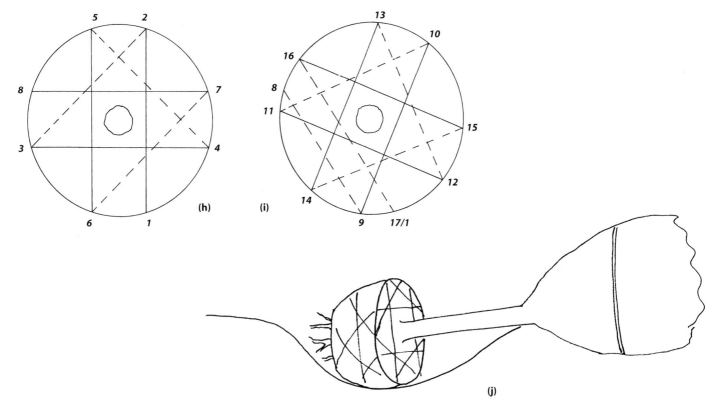

(h) (i)

(j)

8 After you have made one revolution, repeat, 20 degrees out of synch **(i)**. Cross under the rootball from point **8** to point **9**, and then continue. When you have worked the whole way around, tie off at the start point **(17/1)**.

7 The rootball is now ready for the final undercut. Push gently on the trunk, and cut the remaining soil and roots from underneath. Lower the tree slowly to the ground, and then tidy up the bottom of the rootball, cutting any roots that stick out **(j)**.

Provided the tree is being replanted soon, and is not being moved far, this procedure should be enough to contain the soil around the roots. If it is very sunny, or if there is a dry wind, be sure to cover the rootball with sacking immediately. When planting, do not be misled by the weight of the rootball and presume the tree does not need staking—a good stake provides an anchor that allows the roots to re-establish, and is essential in all tree planting. In Japan, larger trees have three bamboo poles supporting them, in a tripod formation. Whereas for smaller trees it is usually recommended to stake low down, to allow the trunk to develop naturally, on more established trees the priority is anchoring the roots, and this is more effective higher up the trunk.

For display, rootballs are wrapped in straw rather than hessian. To-ji market, Kyoto.

Above: Futoshi Yoshioka, of Asuka Noen, Nara Prefecture.

Below: Futoshi's Junior High School, Nara Prefecture.

I was also lucky enough to spend some time working with Futoshi Yoshioka at the Asuka Noen nursery. Asuka itself is a fascinating place, full of ancient burial mounds from the Kofun era (300–710 AD) and what is reckoned to be the first Buddhist temple in Japan, Asuka-dera, built in 596. The nursery covers plots of land all over the village. It grows a range of trees, but is particularly well known for its *Podocarpus macrophyllus*—it was while pruning these that I had my revelation. Futoshi, although still young, was a traditionalist at heart; he played old Japanese folk tunes on his guitar, and was immensely proud of his *uekiya* heritage. He took me to see his Junior High School one day, knowing I would be impressed by the garden. I realized then that as he had been born into an *uekiya* family, and had gone to a school like that one, Futoshi's life was following a predictable pattern.

On leaving Japan, he wrote me a letter, urging me to continue my studies and training, offering these words of advice: "You have to make friends with your tree…you will be able to talk to each tree…you should love nature from your heart, otherwise you cannot make good trees … but most of all you should love your wife."

Niwashi, the Gardeners

The gardeners are the custodians of the remarkable balance between nature—with its cycles, seasons, life and death—and the will and creativity of human beings. Most gardeners work in teams, often under the direction of a designer. Work consists of tending to established gardens as well as building new ones. These gardeners are experienced at moving and placing rocks, laying paths, constructing waterfalls, and a range of other hard landscaping tasks. They tend to have very close working relationships with local nurseries, and their roles are often interchangeable.

I once spent a day helping a gardener and his assistant with the construction of a small private garden (a *tsuboniwa*). A few months later, a particularly bad typhoon hit—and although they were regular customers at the Furukawa nursery, I was surprised when they both turned up and volunteered to help reorganize it. They spent a whole week with us, standing up toppled trees and repairing damage. This flexible approach to work—the community-minded, give-and-take attitude—is typical of traditional Japan, of which nurseries are very much a part.

Left: A trainee gardener at Adachi Art Museum, Shimane Prefecture.

Pruning *Pinus thunbergii* in the *monkaburi* style. Osaka Prefecture.

The team at work, Adachi Art Museum. Shimane Prefecture.

In every team of gardeners there is always a young apprentice. He (traditionally this is a male-dominated profession) might be embarking on a new career, or be a university graduate in landscape design who is learning the practical skills before establishing himself. Often sons of other garden companies or nurseries are sent away for a year to learn the trade before returning to help run their family business. These young men learn from experience and those around them—the older gardeners have a wealth of information to pass on, and there is a strong hierarchy within the group. Until quite recently the new apprentices were not allowed to work on trees in the garden; instead their work was restricted to menial chores such as raking and clearing up, until they were ready for the next step. This has changed, and now they are involved in all aspects of the garden right from the start, although important trees are still reserved for the more experienced gardeners.

While visiting the Adachi Art Museum in Shimane one day in late October, I observed the dynamics of a small gardening team as they gave some pines their autumn tidy-up. They were working closely together; the old head gardener was pruning a small tree, stopping every so often to check on the progress of the others. There was no chatter, but often the younger gardeners would stop and watch their more experienced colleagues, picking up tips and occasionally asking questions. As they stopped for lunch the old man stayed behind, looking closely at each tree, before disappearing for his lunch break too. An hour later they were back, and the boss took a few minutes guiding each assistant through his progress, referring back to his tree as an example.

Gardeners have a great sense of pride in their work. They are respected members of the community, and in turn have a huge amount of respect for their clients and gardens. Anyone who has worked with Japanese gardeners will have a tale to tell, a moment that has stayed with them, that perhaps sums up their experiences. In the fascinating *Secret Teachings In The Art Of Japanese Gardens* (1987), David Slawson recalls an experience he had while training as a gardener in Kyoto: he was reprimanded for working in a clumsy position, for adjusting his weight while squatting on the ground. He describes this moment as bringing about one of the biggest revelations during his training: he realized that even while carrying out seemingly mundane tasks in Japanese gardens (he was sweeping at the time), one must carry oneself properly, with respect for the garden.

My own experience has been uncannily similar. I remember clearing up after a summer pruning of a garden owned by a dentist. Having removed most of the waste, we were having a final sweep, and I casually used my foot to brush some leaves together before scooping them up. I received no reprimand as such—times have changed I suspect—but one of the older

gardeners was quick to stop me, making me squat down and use my hands instead. Scuffing my shoe showed a lack of respect for the garden, even in the final stages of the clean-up. This memory has stayed with me, not as a life-changing moment but as one that made my understanding of the Japanese garden, and indeed Japan in general, more complete.

Anyone who has ever seen gardeners at work in Japan will know that they are quite a sight. Immaculately turned out, in spotless uniforms of khaki shirts and trousers, they nearly always have a hat of some sort—wide-brimmed straw hats, soft floppy hats, or a towel wrapped around the head. Most gardeners wear white work gloves, and on their feet they wear the curious *tabi*, rubber-soled lightweight canvas boots with a separate big toe, giving the impression of a cloven hoof. These *tabi* are soft and flexible, giving good grip for tree climbing and causing less damage to vulnerable moss than ordinary shoes do; construction workers also wear them for working on scaffolding and roofs.

Tools of the Trade

Japanese steel working and blade manufacturing is world famous (think *samurai* swords and kitchen knives), and the garden tools are no exception. Considering all the intricate and varied pruning that takes place throughout each year, it is not surprising that there is a wide range of secateurs, scissors and shears available. *Hasami* (scissors) come in all shapes and sizes for specific jobs, such as the traditional garden scissors (*uekibasami*), spring-action scissors (*mekiribasami*) for bud pruning on pines, and one-handed shears (*hakaribasami*) for clipping topiary. Hedge shears can be long-or short-handled, and the very best are normally the simplest, often without a safety stop to prevent knuckles from hitting on each cut. Japanese saws— well known for cutting on the pull stroke—can be small folding models or larger ones that hang in scabbards from the belt.

Beyond the hand tools, another notable piece of equipment is the aluminium tripod ladder, known as *kyatatsu*. Originally made from bamboo, these are similar to traditional orchard ladders, but more practical and comfortable. Occasionally you see an elaborate scaffolding system of several ladders surrounding a tree, connected with planks high off the ground. These ladders, and the creative ways in which they are put to work, make so much possible in the Japanese garden. For much larger trees, gardeners climb into the crown or are suspended by a crane in special cages, communicating with the ground by radio. Most teams of gardeners, and all nurseries, have at least one crane for this sort of purpose, and for moving rootballed trees.

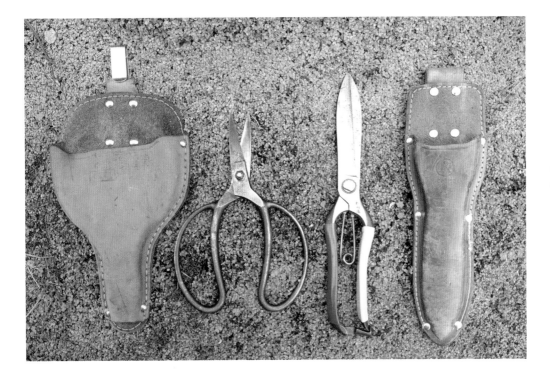

Uekibasami (left) and
hakaribasami (right).

Where to Buy Authentic Tools for *Niwaki*

In my opinion it always pays to get the best tools available, and to look after them. The following are excellent sources of authentic tools:

U.S.A.

Hida Tool & Hardware Co. Inc.,
www.hidatool.com 1-800-443-5512

Stone Lantern / Bonsai Today,
www.stonelantern.com 1-800-776-1167

U.K.

Niwaki,
www.niwaki.com 01243 538395

While good design is of course essential for good gardens, it is the regular upkeep that makes for *fantastic* gardens. It is the work of the *niwashi*, and backstage that of the *uekiya*, that for me defines all Japanese gardens. Their work should never be underestimated.

Kyatatsu tripod ladder.

Japanese–English Plant Names

Written Japanese tends to have fewer spaces between words than written English does. Many of these names are compound words, usually with a prefix to the common species (such as *akamatsu*: *aka* = red, *matsu* = pine). I have resisted the temptation to separate these names, in the hope of providing a more accurate list for reference. The suffix *noki* (literally: 'type of tree') is often used, but again I have excluded it where it is unnecessary. The translation of the Japanese names remains open to interpretation, and I have only included those that I consider useful or interesting.

Akagashi (red oak): *Quercus acuta*

Akamatsu (red pine): *Pinus densiflora*

Biwa: *Eriobotrya japonica*

Chabohiba: *Chamaecyparis obtusa* var. *breviramea*

Daisugi (*dai* = base): *Cryptomeria japonica* (usually) var. *radicans*

Daimochi (*dai* = base): *Ilex integra*

Egonoki: *Styrax japonica*

Enoki: *Celtis sinensis*

Fuji: *Wisteria floribunda*

Ginmokusei (*gin* = silver, describing the white flowers; *mokusei* = osmanthus): *Osmanthus fragrans*

Goyomatsu (five-needled pine): *Pinus parviflora*

Haibyakushin: *Juniperus procumbens*

Hakuren: *Magnolia denudata*

Hanamizuki: *Cornus florida*

Hiiragi: *Osmanthus heterophyllus*

Himarayasugi (phonetic translation of 'Himalayan cedar'): *Cedrus deodara*

Hinoki: *Chamaecyparis obtusa*

Hiyokuhiba: *Chamaecyparis pisifera* 'Filifera'

Hoteichiku (pot-bellied bamboo, referring to the fattened nodes at the base): *Phyllostachys aurea*

Ibuki: *Juniperus chinensis*

Ichii (*ichi* = 1, possible reference to the importance placed on this tree in imperial ceremony): *Taxus cuspidata*

Icho (duck foot, from the Chinese *ya chio*, referring to the leaf shape): *Ginkgo biloba* (The botanical name comes, it is thought, from the bad handwriting of Kaempfer, who introduced the tree from Japan. An early Japanese name was *ginkyo* (silver apricot, after the fruit) but his *y* was misread as a *g* in his notes.)

Inumaki: *Podocarpus macrophyllus*

Inutsuge: *Ilex crenata*

Irohamomiji: *Acer palmatum*

Itozakura: *Prunus pendula* 'Pendula'

Kaede (possibly from *kaeru*, frog, referring to leaf shape/webbed feet): *Acer* species

Kaizuka: *Juniperus chinensis* 'Kaizuka'

Kaki: *Diospyros kaki*

Kashi: *Quercus* species

Katsura: *Cercidiphyllum japonicum*

Keyaki: *Zelkova serrata*

Kinmokusei (gold osmanthus): *Osmanthus fragrans* var. *aurantiacus*

Kiri: *Paulownia tomentosa*

Kitayamasugi: (Kitayama, literally 'North Mountains', an area north of Kyoto): *Cryptomeria japonica* var. *radicans*

Kobushi: *Magnolia kobus*

Koyamaki (Koya is an area in Wakayama): *Sciadopitys verticillata*

Kurochiku (black bamboo): *Phyllostachys nigra*

Kuromatsu (black pine): *Pinus thunbergii*

Kusu: *Cinnamomum camphora*

Kyaraboku: *Taxus cuspidata* var. *nana*

Madake: *Phyllostachys bambusoides*

Maki: *Podocarpus* species (see *inumaki, rakanmaki*)

Matebashi: *Lithocarpus edulis*

Matsu: *Pinus* species (see *akamatsu, goyomatsu, kuromatsu*), also used to imply conifers in general, much as the vague term 'fir tree' is used)

Mikan: *Citrus unshiu*

Mochi: *Ilex integra*

Mokkoku: *Ternstroemia gymnanthera*

Mokuren: *Magnolia liliflora*

Mokusei: *Osmanthus* species

Momi: *Abies firma*

Momiji: *Acer palmatum*

Mosochiku: *Phyllostachys edulis*

Narihiradake: *Semiarundinaria fastuosum*

Ogatamanoki: *Michelia compressa*

Omomiji (big maple, referring to the leaf): *Acer palmatum* var. *amoenum*

Oribu (phonetic translation of 'olive'): *Olea europa*

Rakanmaki: *Podocarpus macrophyllus* var. *maki*

Rengetsutsuji: *Rhododendron japonicum*

Sakaki: *Cleyera japonica*

Sakura: flowering cherry

Sarusuberi (monkey slips, referring to the smooth bark): *Lagerstroemia indica*

Satsuki (the fifth month in the old Japanese calendar, now June, the flowering season): *Rhododendron indicum*

Satozakura: flowering cherry hybrids

Sazanka: *Camellia sasanqua*

Semperu (phonetic translation of 'semper'): *Sequoia sempervirens*

Shi: *Castanopsis cuspidata* var. *sieboldii*

Shidareume (*shidare* = weeping): *Prunus mume* 'Pendula'

Shidareyanagi (*shidare* = weeping): *Salix babylonica*

Shidarezakura (*shidare* = weeping): *Prunus pendula* 'Pendula'

Shirakashi (white oak): *Quercus myrsinifolia*

Someiyoshino: *Prunus ×yedoensis*

Sugi (from *masugu*, or 'straight', referring to the trunk): *Cryptomeria japonica*

Sugigoke (cryptomeria moss): *Polytrichum commune*

Tabunoki: *Machilus thunbergii*

Tonezumimochi: *Ligustrum lucidum*

Tsuga: *Tsuga sieboldii*

Tsubaki: *Camellia japonica*

Tsubarajii: *Castanopsis cuspidata*

Tsuge: *Buxus macrophylla* var. *japonica* (note the shared name with *inutsuge, Ilex crenata*)

Tsutsuji: *Rhododendron obtusum*

Ume: *Prunus mume*

Yamatsutsuji (mountain azalea): *Rhododendron kaempferi*

Yamaboshi (*yama* = mountain, *boshi* = monk): *Cornus kousa*

Yamamomiji (mountain maple): *Acer palmatum* var. *matsumurae*

Yamamomo (mountain peach, referring to the fruit): *Myrica rubra*

Yamazakura (mountain cherry): *Prunus jamasakura*

Yukari (phonetic translation of 'eucaly'): *Eucalyptus* species

Yuzuriha (*yuzuru*, to hand over, referring to the old evergreen leaves that only drop when the new flush opens): *Daphniphyllum macropodum*

Glossary of Japanese Terms

Akadama: reddish clay used for rooting cuttings, and as a growing medium for moss and *bonsai*.

Bonsai: pot-grown trees, trained and pruned to represent those growing in the wild.

Byobu: folding screens.

Byobumatsu: style of pine tree, based on images from *byobu* screens.

Chirashi: pruning technique, where branches and foliage are thinned, rather than shaped.

Chokukanshitate: straight trunk.

Danzukuri: pruning style of branches resembling steps.

Edabukishitate: pruning technique of branches resembling puffs of smoke, or clouds.

Edasukashishitate: pruning technique similar to *chirashi*, involving thinning to preserve the natural habit of the foliage.

Engawa: veranda around traditional Japanese homes and temple buildings.

Edo era: 1600–1867 AD.

Fengshui: Chinese philosophy of geomancy, used to build gardens according to auspicious guidelines.

Fujidana: the training of *Wisteria* species over a trellis or pergola.

Fukinaoshi: the cutting back of a tree to make a new shape.

Fusezukuri: the training of branches (usually pines) over a scaffolding frame.

Hakaribasami: one-handed topiary shears.

Hakomatsu: pines pruned into square, box-like shapes, as at Ritsurin-koen.

Hakozukuri: pruning plants into square shapes, as at Ritsurin-koen.

Hanami: cherry blossom viewing.

Haru ichiban: the first day of spring.

Hasami: scissors.

Ikebana: Japanese flower arranging.

Kadomatsu: New Year arrangement of pine branches.

Kaizukuri: pruning style of branches resembling cockle shells.

Kami: spirits of the Shinto religion.

Karesansui: dry-style garden, made using rocks and gravel.

Karikomi: the clipping of trees and shrubs, usually evergreen azaleas.

Katanagareshitate: one-sided branch style; technique of training one branch out sideways.

Kawaramono: riverbank people; manual labourers from Kyoto, who lived on the riverbanks.

Kobushishitate: pruning technique similar to pollarding, often used on *Lagerstroemia indica*.

Kokarikomi: individual plants clipped into small *karikomi*.

Koyo: autumn colour, particularly of *Acer* species.

Kyatatsu: tripod ladder.

Kyokukanshitate: tree grown with a bendy trunk.

Mame bonsai: very small *bonsai*.

Matsuyani: pine resin.

Meiji Restoration: the return of power to the Emperor Meiji from the Shoguns, 1868–1912 AD.

Mekiribasami: bud-pruning scissors.

Midoritsumi: bud pruning on pines in the late spring.

Mizubachi: mound of earth built up around newly planted trees, to retain water.

Momiage: the thinning of pines in the autumn.

Momoyama era: 1576–1600 AD.

Monkaburi: the branch of a tree, often a pine, trained over a gateway.

Nagareedashitate: an irregular, meandering branch or trunk on a tree.

Nageshinoeda: the branch of a tree, usually a pine, trained over water.

Namikarikomi: plants clipped to represent waves.

Nemaki: wrapping of rootballs, with hessian or straw.

Nemawashi: rootballing.

Niwashi: gardener.

Okarikomi: the clipping of groups of plants into large shapes.

Roji: tea garden, literally meaning 'dewy path'.

Saikai: the growing of miniature landscapes in pots.

Sakutei-ki: eleventh-century manuscript on garden design principals.

Sanzonseki: rock formation based on the Buddhist trilogy of heaven, man and earth.

Sensui kawaramono: early gardeners, developing out of *kawaramono*.

Shakkei: the practice of using distant views within the design.

Shidare: weeping form of trees.

Shimenawa: rope tied around trees and rocks, marking them as sacred in Shinto belief.

Shinto: native Japanese religion.

Sho-chiku-bai: pine-bamboo-Japanese apricot; plants of New Year, often used as a rating system.

Shoyojurin: native evergreen woodland.

Shuronawa: palm-fibre rope, often dyed black.

Sokanshitate: double-trunked trees.

Sozu: bamboo deer scarer.

Takanshitate: tree with many branches.

Takeyabu: bamboo grove.

Tamazukuri: pruning technique of rounded branches.

Tokonoma: alcove in family home.

Tsuboniwa: courtyard garden.

Tsukubai: water basin.

Uekibasami: round-handled scissors.

Uekiya: nursery worker.

Wabi sabi: Japanese aesthetic.

Waramaki: the wrapping of plants for winter protection.

Yukitsuri: supporting branches from the weight of snow.

References

Funakoshi, Rouji. 1992. *Zukai Niwaki no Teire Kotsu no Kotsu* [*Illustrated Guide to Niwaki Skills*]. Tokyo: Nobunkyo.

Gooding, Mel, and William Furlong. 2002. *Song of the Earth*. London: Thames and Hudson.

Hillier Nurseries. 1998. *The Hillier Manual of Trees and Shrubs*. Newton Abbot, Devon: David and Charles.

Hisamatsu, Shinichi. 1971. *Zen and the Fine Arts*. Tokyo: Kodansha.

Infojardin. 2005. http://www.infojardin.net Accessed 13 January 2006.

Itoh, Teiji. 1984. *The Gardens of Japan*. Tokyo: Kodansha.

Juniper, Andrew. 2003. *Wabi Sabi: The Japanese Art of Impermanence*. Boston: Tuttle Publishing.

Keene, Donald. 1967. *Essays in Idleness: The Tsurezuregusa of Kenko*. New York: Columbia University Press.

Kitamura, Fumio, and Yurio Ishizu. 1963. *Garden Plants in Japan*. Tokyo: Kokusai Bunka Shinkokai.

Kuitert, Wybe. 1988. *Themes, Scenes and Taste in the History of Japanese Garden Art*. Amsterdam: J. C. Gieben.

Levy-Yamamori, Ran, and Gerard Taaffe. 2004. *Garden Plants Of Japan*. Portland, Oregon: Timber Press.

Nitschke, Gunter. 1993. *Japanese Gardens*. Cologne: Benedickt Taschen.

Nose, Michiko Rico, and Michael Freeman. 2002. *The Modern Japanese Garden*. Boston: Tuttle Publishing.

Ota, Katsusuke, and Takeshi Asou. 1999. *Hajimete no Niwaki no Sentei to Seishi* [*Introduction to Pruning and Shaping Niwaki*]. Tokyo: Nihonbungeisha.

Rowthorn, Chris, John Ashburn, Sara Benson, and Mason Florence. 2000. *Japan*. Victoria, Australia: Lonely Planet Publications.

The Royal Horticultural Society *Plant Finder*. 2006. *Chamaecyparis obtusa*. http://rhs.org.uk/rhsplantfinder/asp Accessed 10 March 2006.

Schaal, Hans Dieter. 1994. *Landscape as Inspiration*. Berlin: Ernest and Sohn.

Slawson, David. 1987. *Secret Teachings in the Art of Japanese Gardens*. Tokyo: Kodansha.

Stryk, Lucien. 1985. *On Love and Barley: Haiku of Basho*. London: Penguin.

Tsukushi, Nobuzane. 1964. *Amaterasu no Tanjo* [*The Birth of the Sun God*]. Tokyo: Kadogawa Shinsho.

Yama-Kei Publishers. 1985. *Nihon no Jyumoku* [*Garden Plants of Japan*]. Tokyo: Yama-Kei Publishers.

Yamashita, Yukata. 1989. *Shippaishinai Niwaki no Teire, Seishi to Sentei* [*How to Prune and Shape Niwaki*]. Tokyo: Seibidoshyuppan.

Index

Page numbers in **boldface** indicate photographs or illustrations.

A

Abies firma, 100
Acer
  japonicum, 40, 109
  palmatum, 38, **108**, 109-112, **110**, **112**, 118
    'Dissectum', **109**
    var. *amoenum*, 109
    var. *matsumurae*, 109
    var. *palmatum*, 109
  shirasawanum, 109
Acorus gramineus, 122
Adachi Art Museum, 32, **33**, **47**, **64**, 67, **68**, **78**, 133
akagashi. See Quercus acuta
akamatsu. See Pinus densiflora
Anraku-ji, **47**
apical dominance, 55
Architectural Plants, **43**, **105**
ash. See *Fraxinus excelsior*
Asuka Noen, **132**
Aucuba japonica, 33, 34
auxin, 45
azalea. See *Rhododendron*

B

bamboo, 119-121
Basho, 81, 112
beech. See *Fagus*
biwa. See Eriobotrya japonica
black pine. See *Pinus thunbergii*
bonsai, 27, 36, **43**, 44, **89**, 111
box. See *Buxus*
Buddhism, 20
Buxus, 107, 128
  macrophylla, 37, 82
    var. *japonica*, 137
  sempervirens, 27, 34, 50, **107**
byobu, 29, 35, 63
byobumatsu, 29, **35**

C

Camellia, 106
  sasanqua, 106
  japonica, 33, 49, 101, **106**
Castanopsis, 20
  cuspidata, 40, 101, 102
    var. *sieboldii*, 102
Cedrus deodara, **25**, 29, **97-98**
Celtis chinensis, 118
Cercidiphyllum japonicum, 22, 118

Cercis chinensis, 22
chabohiba. See Chamaecyparis obtusa 'Breviramea'
Chamaecyparis, 96
  obtusa, 14, 22, 85, 93, 99
    'Breviramea', 99, **100**
  pisifera 'Filifera', 99
China, 23, 26
chirashi, 30, 97
Chishaku-in, **33**
chokukanshitate, 27
Chrysanthemum grandiflorum, **122**, 123
Cinnamomum camphora, **44**, 107
Cleyera japonica, 107
Cornus
  florida, 118
  kousa, 40, 118
Crepe myrtle. See *Lagerstroemia indica*
Cryptomeria, 20
  japonica, 14, 22, 38, 43, 85-90, 99, **104**, 106, 123
    'Elegans', 86
    'Globulosa Nana', 86
    var. *radicans*, 86-90
×*Cupressocyparis leylandii*, 49, 96
Cupressus, 49
  glabra, **43**, 96
  macrocarpa, 95, **96**
Cycas revoluta, **24**, 25

D

daimochi, 31, **105**
Daisen-in, **21**, 66
daisugi, 86-90
Daitoku-ji, 87
danzukuri, 27, **28**
Daphniphyllum macropodum, 107
Diospyros kaki, 15
Dutch rush. See *Equisetum hymale*

E

edabukishitate, 27
edasukashishitate, **97**
egonoki. See Styrax japonica
engawa, 30, 31
enoki. See Celtis sinensis
Equisetum hymale, 79, 122
Eriobotrya japonica, 107
Eucalyptus, 29, 107, 129
Euonymous japonicus, 49

F

Fagus
  crenata, 109
  sylvatica, 34
Fatsia japonica, 33, 34